Bold Women in Michigan History

BY VIRGINIA LAW BURNS

2006

Mountain Press Publishing Company
Missoula, Montana

Cover art © 2006 Michael-Che Swisher
On front cover: Magdelaine LaFramboise, fur trader
On back cover (*top*): Sippie Wallace, the Detroit Nightingale;
(*below*) Pearl Kendrick and Grace Eldering, chief inventors of the
pertussis and DPT vaccines

Definition of "bold" (back cover) from *Merriam-Webster's
Collegiate Dictionary,* 11th edition (2003).

Library of Congress Cataloging-in-Publication Data
Burns, Virginia.
   Bold women in Michigan history / by Virginia Law Burns.
     p. cm.
   Includes bibliographical references and index.
   ISBN 0-87842-525-X (pbk. : alk. paper)
   1. Women—Michigan—Biography. I. Title.
CT241.B87 2006
977.4'0430922—dc22
[B]
                                       2006023139

*Printed in the United States of America by
Data Reproductions Corporation, Auburn Hills, Michigan*

Mountain Press Publishing Company
P.O. Box 2399
Missoula, MT 59806
406-728-1900

To the bold women
of today and tomorrow!
and

Evelyn —
all good wishes in
your writing

Virginia Law Burns

Contents

Acknowledgments

WHEN MY SOUTHERN-BORN FRIEND PEGGY was feeling grateful toward someone, she used to say, "If I'da been a dog, I'da licked that gal's face." During research on this book, I often shared that feeling.

My new projects always start with tried-and-true friends like Gladys Beckwith, founder and director of the Michigan Women's Historical Center and Hall of Fame in Lansing. Vicci Knowlton and Katie Cavanaugh at the Center were also extraordinary helps. Michigan historian Geneva Wiskemann was one of my lifelines as always, and sister writer Jean Pitrone helped generally as well as being my most valuable resource for the profile of Myra Wolfgang. My delightful daughter Meg Kittleson was an invaluable teacher and comforter when the computer and I were at an impasse. My son, Jim Ritchie, found exactly the blues lyric needed for the Wallace chapter. Carrie Dreager helped get me started, and friend Judy Malitz proofread the first draft. Editor Beth Judy posed hundreds of good questions and led me patiently and skillfully through many rough places.

Others who contributed include Sandra Chavez, head librarian at Laingsburg Library; also librarians Brenda Davidson, Julie Pierce, Eliza George, Cynthia Lara, Mary Hennessey, Amee Purosky, Tracie Kreighbaum, Lauren Douglass, Janice Murphy, Wendy Flowenoy, Sarah Lopshan, Kris Rzepenzynski, Edwina Morgan, Karon White, Gloriane Peck, Kate Pohjola, Cynthia Terwilliger, Marcia Young, Rayna Bohm and Kathyrn at the Bloomfield Hills Library, and countless others. Librarians, I salute you!

Specific to the Chandler/Haviland chapter, special thanks to author Marcia Mason; Charles Lindquist, who provided detailed data; and Christopher Haviland. For the Gillette chapter, Christopher

Graham, Dave Dempsey, Phyllis Hickman, and Trisha Belcher offered generous help. Carolyn Shapiro provided inspiration for the Kendrick/Eldering chapter, and Bill Crafts at the Michigan State Laboratories sent invaluable material. David Armour critiqued the LaFramboise chapter; the Harbour View Inn on Mackinac Island sent materials and allowed us to reproduce their painting of Magdelaine; and Judith Stewart graciously allowed use of photographs in memory of her husband, Don Gentner. John Beutler with the Michigan Senate provided critical information about Cora Brown just as I was beginning to despair. Thanks to Marygrove College, especially Rene Prewit and Tresa Meyer, for the photo of Madame Cadillac's statue, and to Annick Hivert-Carthew for primary source material on the Cadillac family. Candace Eaton at the Petoskey Museum; Joe Mitchell of the Little Traverse Bay Band of Odawas; and Robert and Linda Dominic were invaluable for the chapter on Waunetta Dominic. Martha Wolfgang helped with the chapter on her mother, Myra Wolfgang.

Through the years I have been a devotee of all things Michigan. In time, a vision grew and stretched for me: I would publish stories about Michigan's poorly recognized heroic women—women who acted on their yearning to improve the human condition.

I had to limit the number of women I could feature in this book. I sincerely hope that you are inspired by those I chose.

1 Fort Pontchartrain, home of Marie-Thérèse Cadillac
2 Childhood home of Magdelaine LaFramboise
3 Trading post and southern home of Magdelaine LaFramboise
4 Mackinac Island home of Magdelaine LaFramboise
5 Home of Elizabeth Chandler and Laura Haviland
6 Home of Emma Edmonds
7 Home of Lucy Thurman
8 Birthplace of Marguerite deAngeli
9 Home of Pearl Kendrick and Grace Eldering
10 Childhood home of Genevieve Gillette
11 Home of Genevieve Gillette
12 Home of Sippie Wallace
13 Home of Cora Brown
14 Home of Myra Wolfgang
15 Home of Waunetta Dominic
16 Home of Delia Villegas Vorhauer

Statue of Marie-Thérèse Cadillac at Marygrove College, Detroit —photo by Dirk Bakker

Marie-Thérèse Cadillac

BOLD WOMAN OF NEW FRANCE

ON THE NORTH BANK of the great St. Lawrence River in Quebec, a small village perched in the wilderness. It was the seventeenth century. Settlers in New France, as Canada and northern parts of the United States were called at that time, had founded Beauport as a trading village. Here, people came to sell and buy furs—especially, beaver.

Some of Beauport's first settlers were the Guyons, who came over from France in 1634 and became prosperous. Denis Guyon, a shipping merchant, married Elizabeth Boucher, who had blood ties to the French royal family, and they had at least two boys, Michel-Denis and Jacques. Then in April 1671, Elizabeth had a third child, a baby girl named Marie-Thérèse ("Thérèse" is pronounced tay-REZZ).

Growing up in a fur-trading village, Marie-Thérèse learned all about swapping goods—for example, blankets, cloth, and sugar—for smelly but valuable beaver pelts. She played with children from Indian tribes who lived and traveled in the area—the Abenacki, whose name means "People of the Dawn Land"; the Huron, who had an extensive trade empire; and the Iroquois, who traded mainly with the Dutch. In a trade town, Marie-Thérèse was exposed to all kinds of people: the Indians who came with furs; Frenchmen who also hunted, trapped, and traded, known as *coureurs de bois* (pronounced CURR-er da BWAH), or "woods runners"; and the Europeans and others who sailed to New France to buy furs.

Surrounded by trade and adventure, Marie-Thérèse may have dreamed of running away and becoming a coureur de bois herself. In the seventeenth century in New France, however, women of European descent had few options when it came to lifestyle. Legally and within the church, they were under men's control. Their lives consisted mainly of bearing and raising children and managing their families. However, more than many other women of her time, Marie-Thérèse would live her life combining traditional expectations with spirited adventure—including a journey that would make a coureur de bois proud. She succeeded in many worlds—in high society, in the wilderness, and in other venues her life would take her to.

When Marie-Thérèse was around twelve, her mother died. In spring 1683, Marie-Thérèse's father took her to Quebec City, about thirty miles south, where she entered a boarding school run by nuns at the Ursuline monastery. Her classmates included Huron, Iroquois, and Abenacki girls whose parents had become rich in the fur trade. To communicate with these girls and their families, the nuns spoke several native languages. Life at the Ursuline school was rigorous. Being late for class or speaking out of turn could result in hours of drudgery in the washhouse, scrubbing bedding, washing the nuns' shapeless blue gowns, or starching their wide, white collars and veils.

Marie-Thérèse's best friend, Anne Picote de Belestre, also went to the Ursuline school. They made a handsome pair: Marie-Thérèse, with her heavy, dark brown hair and flashing eyes, and mild, fair-haired Anne. Students at the Ursuline school wore long, loose, blue dresses with a white kerchief knotted at the throat. A white bonnet, which the girls hated, completed the uniform.

Scholastically, Marie-Thérèse was an average student. In addition to academic subjects, the girls were instructed in sewing, embroidery, art appreciation, and painting. They learned good manners, up-to-date French court dances, and how to play the harpsichord and recorder. Outside of class, the girls probably practiced fan language, high society's "secret code" used at parties and balls in France. For example, holding a fan in the left hand, opening it wide, and covering one's face with it up to the eyes was a way to say, "I want to get to know you." Touching the handle to the lips meant, "Kiss me."

In 1685, when Marie-Thérèse was fourteen, her father died. An orphan now, she remained in school. But she was reaching the age when Quebec society expected girls to become engaged or to marry.

Marie-Thérèse's uncle, François Guyon, was a privateer off the coast of New France. His job was to protect the coast by stopping foreign ships and inspecting and sometimes confiscating their cargo. In Acadia, the easternmost part of New France, Guyon became impressed with a young man named Antoine Laumont de la Mothe Cadillac, originally from southwest France. There is some dispute about Cadillac's true origins, but a military career in the French army probably brought him to the European "New World." Some historians think that, when he started over in North America, Antoine invented a different background for himself, complete with an aristocratic name and family shield—seen, much later, on Cadillac automobiles. Whatever his true heritage, he was energetic and full of ideas for New France. Guyon invited Antoine to sail with him, and through her uncle, Marie-Thérèse met her future husband.

Antoine was thirteen years older than Marie-Thérèse. The son of a judge, his manner was bold and straightforward. Smooth-talking and well-schooled, he also possessed a wicked sense of humor. He was charismatic; people noticed and remembered him. In part that was because he was handsome, with black hair curling freely around his square jaw, a narrow mustache under a hawk-like nose, and a smile that charmed birds out of trees. Working out of Port Royal, Acadia (now Annapolis Royal, Nova Scotia), Antoine became known as an excellent maritime navigator who knew the coasts of both New France and New England very well.

According to legend, the romance between Marie-Thérèse and Antoine ignited at a ball in Quebec City's huge, stone-faced Chateau St. Louis in spring 1687. The courtship ended that summer in a wedding in Beauport. Marie-Thérèse was sixteen. Antoine was twenty-nine.

The couple began married life in Acadia. Working out of Port Royal, Antoine developed trade contacts, explored the wilderness of New France, and recruited other young explorers. He was also something of a spy for New France, keeping an eye on British settlers who were also profiting from fur trading. The British and the French were intense rivals for the riches and rule of Canada. Already there had been skirmishes and battles.

Near Port Royal, the couple lived in a little vertical-log cabin on fine cleared land. Gaspard, an Abenacki teen, lived with them. Antoine had bought Gaspard's freedom from an Iroquois war party that had captured him. In gratitude, he worked on the farm and kept a protective eye on his rescuer's family. By spring 1689, Marie-Thérèse and Antoine had two children, Judith and Joseph. Antoine's work often took him away from home for long periods of time. In 1689, he was even called to France to help plan a sea attack against New England. The French king Louis and the minister of the colonies, Pontchartrain, were impressed with the young Cadillac.

During the spring of 1690, when Antoine was away on a trip, Gaspard came running to find Marie-Thérèse. English warships with troops from Massachusetts were sailing up the river toward Port Royal! Marie-Thérèse bundled up the children and packed provisions, and the little party of four raced for the woods. For three weeks they hid. At last, Gaspard circled back to Port Royal to investigate. The village had surrendered. The soldiers had practically destroyed the Cadillacs' farm. With nowhere else to go, Gaspard, Marie-Thérèse, and the children began making their way back to Quebec City, where her brothers lived.

They had just managed to hitch a ride on a French battleship when a fast Spanish pirate ship captured the French brig. Quick-thinking Gaspard leaped overboard during the takeover, but Marie-Thérèse, holding Judith and Joseph close, had to stay and face the pirate captain. He turned out to be polite, and she arranged for her ransom to be paid by her brothers in Quebec. Alerted by Gaspard, her brothers were waiting when Marie-Thérèse and the children were dropped off in Quebec City. After this incident, there is no record of what became of Gaspard.

Living in Quebec City now, Marie-Thérèse renewed her connection with her old friend Anne, now married to Alphonse de Tonti, and had two more children, little Antoine and Magdalene. For his part, the elder Antoine was becoming friends with the French governor of North America, Louis de Buade Frontenac. Antoine seems to have been able to gain favor with people in power. By now, Marie-Thérèse knew her husband well. He had great ambitions for France and its control of North America, and he had great personal ambition, too. He saw nothing wrong in combining the two. His self-interest would bring wealth to his family, but it would also earn him enemies and trouble.

In 1694, Governor Frontenac gave Antoine a post to command: Fort de Buade, near St. Ignace in present-day Michigan's Upper Peninsula, not far from Mackinac Island. The fort, strategically located at a narrowing of land known as a strait, lay between Lake Huron and Lake Michigan. At Fort de Buade, Antoine was supposed to track English movements in New France and ensure stable relations with the native tribes there.

Marie-Thérèse knew a primitive fort would be too hard for their children. When Antoine went to Fort de Buade, Marie-Thérèse moved her family to Montreal. There, while nursing a new baby, she became Antoine's *commissaire* or purchasing agent, buying all the provisions and equipment the fort needed. Marie-Thérèse's business sense and organizational skills lifted a major responsibility from Antoine.

By 1697, Governor Frontenac ordered troops to withdraw from Fort de Buade and other French trading forts. Catholic priests had complained about terrible behavior among the Indians at the forts, behavior the priests felt Antoine encouraged by allowing alcohol. There were economic reasons for the closures as well. Thus Antoine came home. But he had a new plan. Marie-Thérèse listened as he laid out his dream of building a new trading fort in an even better location: another narrowing of land between Lake Huron and Lake Erie, known in French as *le détroit,* or "the strait."

Antoine convinced his old friend Frontenac and even the French king that a fort was needed at "Detroit." King Louis granted Antoine twelve acres on the wide, swift-flowing Detroit River. The explorer and trader in Antoine rejoiced. He began to assemble a crew of adventurers. In Montreal on June 4, 1701, Marie-Thérèse and the children waved goodbye to Antoine and nine-year-old Antoine, who was accompanying his father. Twenty-five canoes, packed and ready, floated on the St. Lawrence River. Between one hundred and two hundred soldiers, colonists, friendly tribesmen, and missionaries milled about. Alphonse de Tonti, Anne's husband, was Antoine's second in command. Ahead lay a journey of almost two months. At the end of July, the party would arrive and begin building Fort Pontchartrain on the future site of Detroit.

When Antoine left, Marie-Thérèse, now thirty years old, was pregnant again. She and Antoine agreed that after the baby was born and the fort had houses and other necessary buildings, he would send for her and the children. Just three days after his departure, the baby was born—a girl whom Marie-Thérèse named after her friend Anne. But two days later, baby Anne died. Perhaps the death spurred Marie-Thérèse's resolve not to wait for Antoine to send for her. She began organizing a wilderness party for Detroit. The party included her friend Anne de Tonti.

Marie-Thérèse flew about, using her experience as a purchasing agent to pull the expedition together. She hired a guide and decided on the route. Together Anne and Marie-Thérèse sewed deerskin clothing for themselves and their children, though for now, Marie-Thérèse's daughters Judith and Magdalene would stay at the Ursuline school.

When the day came, Marie-Thérèse kissed her daughters goodbye on the Montreal pier. She and her sons climbed into huge canoes, tucking themselves among possessions and trade goods. In another canoe she could see Anne and Anne's brother, François. It was the first week of September 1701.

As they crossed the length of Lake Frontenac, now Lake Ontario. Marie-Thérèse and Anne both took turns with the paddle. It grew cold at night, and autumn rains began. At the end of the lake thundered Niagara Falls. They would have to portage around it. For several days, the party worked to carry everything, even the canoes, for ten miles around the falls. Though small, Marie-Thérèse and Anne did their parts, struggling into backpacks weighing between fifty and seventy-five pounds and hand-carrying their paddles.

A priest who crossed paths with the party later described how he expressed concern for Marie-Thérèse's safety. She replied, "When a woman loves her husband, no place where he is can be dangerous." Marie-Thérèse and Anne had chosen to follow their men on their own terms, and they may have greatly enjoyed the trip. After all, few European women of their time had such an opportunity for adventure.

After the falls, another great lake lay ahead: Erie. They resumed paddling. Soon, however, their guide had to leave. Later, Marie-Thérèse would discover that he had stolen trade goods from them. He would be brought to trial.

They found an Abenacki man to lead them the rest of the way. At last, in mid-October, the party had advanced to a wide river bordered by broad, grassy meadows and wild orchards. They were getting close. Marie-Thérèse and Anne changed from their soiled deerskins into dresses of satin, silk, and lace. Joseph and Jacques put on fresh shirts and pants. Word had been sent ahead, and when the fort came into view, a cannon boomed in welcome.

Fort Pontchartrain sat on a cliff with the river on three sides. A tower rose at each corner of the fort walls. Outside the walls of vertical logs, native encampments clustered about. Their occupants were busy firing muskets in the air in celebration. In the crowd waiting by the fort's water gate, or river door, Marie-Thérèse spotted her husband and young Antoine. Such a joyful reunion for the husband, wife, and three brothers! There were gifts of beads and trade goods for all and, that night in the fort, a feast of bear and venison.

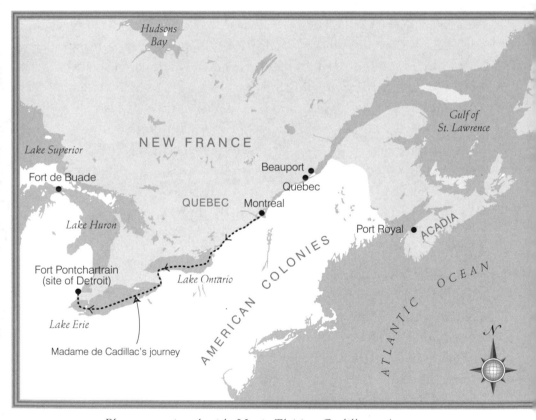

Places associated with Marie-Thérèse Cadillac, 1671–1711, including her 1701 journey to Fort Ponchartrain at Detroit

Marie-Thérèse quickly set up housekeeping in one of the two commander's houses. Anne and Alphonse had the other house. Constructed of vertical logs, the houses had roofs of tree bark. The largest room had a fireplace and a chimney of twigs and mud. Deerskin scraped very thin served as glass in the windows. Over simple floors of pounded earth, Marie-Thérèse laid carpets she had brought.

In the spring, a few more French women braved the thousand-mile journey from Quebec to Fort Pontchartrain, either to join their husbands or to find one there. Fortunately for the growing community, there was an abundance of food. The Detroit River and surrounding forest provided plentiful fish, deer, bear, and fowl. Arriving settlers brought pigs, cattle, and chickens, which reproduced and could be traded. In just a few years, more than six miles of land along the river became cultivated.

Out of necessity, Marie-Thérèse became the fort doctor. Anne helped her friend remember and write down the remedies their mothers and the nuns had used. The women also learned remedies from native men and women, gathered herbs in the woods, and grew garlic.

Marie-Thérèse and Anne were the first white women many of the native people had seen. For some reason, relations between the French and native tribes improved after they arrived. Perhaps it was because both Marie-Thérèse and Anne had grown up with Indian neighbors and schoolmates, and natives found them easier to get along with than some Europeans. Sadly for the two friends, however, the relationship between their husbands was deteriorating. A struggle for power simmered between the two men, and their wives could do nothing about it.

In November 1702, Cadillac canoed back to Quebec and returned with Joseph and Magdalene. Judith stayed at the Ursuline monastery. At the fort, Marie-Thérèse and Anne taught French, religion, and sewing to mixed classes of French and Indian children. In 1704, a fire burned their houses down, but they rebuilt. Over the ten years that the Cadillacs stayed at Fort Pontchartrain, Marie-Thérèse had five or six more children. Only three of them survived to adulthood. In all, over the course of twenty-one years, she bore thirteen children, seven of whom survived.

Trade at the fort flourished, and Antoine's own pockets grew full. Since he owned land at the fort, he could collect rent for the cabins within the fort's walls, as well as on the lands beyond. Fees for fur-trapping licenses became his profit also. In 1706, Antoine prevailed in the long power struggle with Alphonse de Tonti, and de Tonti was recalled to Quebec. The parting of the two friends, Marie-Thérèse and Anne, must have been very sad. As before, Marie-Thérèse helped Antoine purchase supplies, and whenever he returned to Quebec on business, she ran the fort. Clearly Antoine, a man who liked to be in control, respected and trusted his wife's skills and judgment.

However, in 1711, the French minister had enough of Antoine's desire for power. In addition, his business dealings often seemed questionable, causing complaints and ill will. Antoine was discharged from Fort Pontchartrain and demoted to the post of governor of Louisiana. For a few years, the Cadillacs made a new home in a fort near present-day Mobile, Alabama (which was part of Louisiana at that time). The living situation was entirely different from what they were used to, with a hot climate, unfriendly Indians, starvation, and disease. In addition, Antoine lost much of his land in New France when the English conquered it. After four years in Louisiana, he was recalled to France.

France! Much as she might have dreamed of it as a child, Marie-Thérèse had never lived there. She was French-Canadian, not French. But the family received a welcome that was far less than warm. Upon his arrival in Paris, Antoine and his son Joseph spent five months in the Bastille prison charged with treason, while Marie-Thérèse and the other children lived on borrowed money in the town of La Rochelle. Later, Antoine and Joseph were released, and Antoine received a medal for wrongful imprisonment. For the last eight years of his life, Antoine lived comfortably as the governor of Castelsarrasin, a city near his hometown. He died at age seventy-two. Marie-Thérèse lived sixteen more years after his death. She was buried in 1746 in France.

At the end of her life, there in southern France, did she dream of cold lakes, canoes, and forts in the wilderness? We will never know. We do know that she helped found the city of Detroit, that she and her best friend were the first European women in Michigan, and that she had the first surviving white child born in Detroit—named Marie-Thérèse, like her mother. Combining a traditional French heritage with her New French upbringing, Marie-Thérèse Cadillac made a home for herself, her family, and her community in the wilderness. As one historian wrote, she was a model of "gracious, competent womanhood"—with a little coureur de bois thrown in.

A painting of Magdelaine LaFramboise based on historical research (no actual photographs or likenesses exist)

—artist, Jian H. Zhang; courtesy Harbour View Inn. Photo, Don Gentner

Magdelaine LaFramboise

FUR TRADER

IN AN ODAWA VILLAGE near the mouth of the Grand River, on the shores of Lake Michigan, Magdelaine Marcot, granddaughter of Chief Returning Cloud, waited for the womenfolk of her tribe to help prepare her for her wedding. Like her mother before her, fourteen-year-old Magdelaine had chosen to marry a French-Canadian fur trader. It was 1794.

Joseph LaFramboise, Magdelaine's intended husband, had paid her family a steep bride price. It is easy to imagine, when the wedding hour arrived, Joseph smiling at his betrothed as she stood straight and self-assured in a soft, fringed deerskin dress, her dark eyes shining. The wedding was a tribal ceremony "in the custom of the country," that is, without priest or legal paperwork, but binding within the tribe.

Though Magdelaine might have felt excited and nervous about her marriage, she had grown up in a community that included fur traders, and surely knew that romance had little to do with Joseph LaFramboise's proposal of marriage. Marriage between traders and native families brought advantages for both husband and wife. It transformed the traders into family, friends, and allies within Indian communities, which depended heavily on fur trapping for their livelihood. Business became more than a formal trading of goods.

For about a century, Michigan had been part of France's North American colony, New France. In the beginning, French soldiers had built log forts in the wild forests, which they guarded against their enemies—first the Spanish and British, with their Indian allies, and later the Americans. Priests came to live within the walls of the forts and traveled among the Indians to convert them to Catholicism. Fur trappers used the forts as a base, and traders like Magdelaine's father bartered skins, mostly beaver, for supplies. People in France bought these furs to resell and became rich.

The Odawa, also known as the Ottawa, were one of the tribes allied with the French. Renowned traders, the Odawa had in fact taken their name from a word in their language meaning "to trade." The tribe lived comfortably, primarily through hunting and trapping. The women were fine agriculturists, with thousands of acres planted with vegetables and apple trees. The Odawa valued the individualism of each tribal member. Women had a voice in their community, and children were cherished by all.

When French explorers and fur trappers came into Odawa territory in the 1600s, the Odawa cemented their trade relations with the newcomers by intermarrying. In the 1770s, Magdelaine's French father, Jean-Baptiste Marcot, and her Odawa mother, Marie, kept up this tradition of intermarriage. They lived at Fort St. Joseph, a trading post near present-day Niles in southwest Michigan. Their first child, Therese, was born in 1776. Magdelaine was born in 1780, and that year the family's life changed dramatically. Fort St. Joseph had passed into British hands, and a new commander in the area decided all French and Indian inhabitants of Fort St. Joseph must leave.

With Magdelaine on a cradleboard, the displaced family moved north and west, on foot and by canoe, into present-day Wisconsin. The uprooting proved to be tragic Between the Fox and Wisconsin Rivers, Indians murdered Jean-Baptiste. In an instant, Marie's life turned upside down. Now husbandless, she returned with her daughters to her home village on the Grand River, near present-day Grand Haven, and raised Magdelaine and Therese among her own Odawa people.

The Odawa lived up and down the coast of Lake Michigan, and especially around Mackinac Island. When Magdelaine was six, Marie took her and Therese to be baptized in St. Anne's Roman Catholic Church on Mackinac Island. It was a long paddle north on the huge lake, but Catholic priests were few in the region; religious ceremonies had to be postponed until a priest came to Mackinac. The island, likened in some tribal legends to a great swimming turtle, lay in the five-mile-wide Straits of Mackinac separating Michigan's upper and lower peninsula.

Ten years after her first marriage ceremony, Magdelaine returned to St. Anne's Church with Joseph to say their Catholic marriage vows. By that time they had a daughter, Josette, born a year after their Odawa marriage, and a son, Joseph, about one year old. In the fur trade, Joseph senior worked as a middleman, running a store at Ada in the Grand River valley, where trappers sold him pelts in exchange for blankets, knives, axes, brass kettles, and other goods he bought at Mackinac. The store at Ada was one of lower Michigan's first permanent trading posts. From spring through fall, Joseph traveled into the forest to trade.

In 1806, history tragically repeated itself in Magdelaine's life. She, Joseph, a servant, and several boatmen were paddling home after a trip to Mackinac Island. Baby Joseph was also with them, but Josette, now ten years old, was away at boarding school in Montreal, Canada. Their large, lightweight boats, called bateaus, were loaded with merchandise. In the afternoon, the party stopped to rest at one of Lake Michigan's pristine beaches. Suddenly, a musket blast shattered the stillness. Joseph senior fell bleeding where he had knelt to say his prayers, dead by the hand of an angry tribesman to whom he had refused to sell liquor earlier that day. The little group could do no more than wrap Joseph's body in blankets and continue on. They buried Magdelaine's husband in Grand Haven, a quarter of a century after her father had died the same way.

Now twenty-six, Magdelaine was a widow with Josette and Joseph to raise. How could she educate them without Joseph's income? She thought about her ability to speak fluent French, English, Odawa, and other Indian languages. She had assisted Joseph as a translator, worked in the store, and traded in his absence. She decided to step into her late husband's role as a fur trader.

From 1806 to 1812, Magdelaine conducted her fur business as an independent trader, the way Joseph had done. Madame LaFramboise, as she was known, rose fast in the business, quickly earning a reputation for her high-quality pelts, her business sense, and her social skills. One of her biggest potential rivals was John Jacob Astor, the powerful businessman and owner of the American Fur Company who had squeezed out many independent fur traders in Canada and newly founded America. But Magdelaine managed to become an employee of Astor and sell him pelts while at the same time maintaining her independence as a Grand River valley trader.

Her job required that she travel often to Mackinac Island to trade. Though she lived in a world peopled more and more by whites and other non-Indians, Magdelaine always dressed in traditional Odawa clothes of soft deerskin, fringed and beaded. Under her shawl, she may have worn a beaded blouse of white cloth, with colorful necklaces encircling her neck and shoulders. On her feet were moccasins, and her dark hair would have been braided, most likely in one braid down the back.

Magdelaine earned at least five times more per year than the average Great Lakes trader. Her success at trading is even more impressive considering that she didn't learn to read or write until she was forty-one years old. Her ability to thrive in many different cultures may have helped her do so well. She was active within Catholic fur-trading society, which included people of various ancestries—the various Great Lakes Indian tribes, Metis (French and Indian, like Magdelaine), French, French-Canadian, and others. The fur traders were the social leaders of their time and place, and as such, Magdelaine and the others entertained lavishly in their elegant homes. At the same time, Magdelaine clung to her Odawa roots and ways and the kinship with her mother's people. Her business success shows that she was comfortable as a woman in a male-dominated business world.

But Magdelaine wasn't the only female fur trader in her community. Her sister, Therese, also worked in the trade. Like Magdelaine, Therese had married at age fourteen, to a French adventurer named LaSalier. The couple had a daughter, but LaSalier disappeared and never returned. In 1804 Therese married again, to Mackinac Island fur trader George Schindler, from whom she learned the business. A friend of Magdelaine and Therese, Elizabeth Bertrand Mitchell, the Metis wife of a doctor and the mother of twelve children, also pursued the trade and was a leader in fur-trading society for fifty years.

In the winter of 1815–1816, twenty-year-old Josette finished boarding school and returned to her mother on Mackinac Island. There, Josette promptly fell in love with an army captain stationed at Fort Mackinac, Benjamin Pierce. (Benjamin's brother Franklin would go on to become president of the United States.) The couple married in April, and soon Magdelaine had a granddaughter, also named Josette.

Sadly, Magdelaine's daughter and a second grandchild, Benjamin, died in 1821. Magdelaine raised her surviving grandchild and provided well for her financially for the rest of her life. Magdelaine's other child, Joseph, later went on to become an interpreter among the Sioux and Ojibwa in Minnesota and establish a trading post there. He married a Metis woman, Jane Dickson.

In 1822, Magdelaine sold her lodge, store, and fur-trading business in the Grand River Valley to Rix Robinson. Rix had been one of the first white settlers in that part of Michigan, and Magdelaine had known and done business with him for years. Married to an Odawa-Ojibwa woman, he was respected among whites and Indians. He became an Indian advocate, a circuit court judge, a Michigan senator, and a supporter of women's right to vote. The home and business Magdelaine had built up would be in good hands.

Magdelaine began to put down permanent roots on Mackinac Island in 1820 when she had a spacious, white frame house built on Huron Street. The house had three floors, with a balcony over the front door. Close to St. Anne's Church, it overlooked the deep, fast-flowing Straits of Mackinac.

It seemed as if Magdelaine had built her house large in order to have room for her community. In 1823, Reverend William Ferry, a Presbyterian minister, asked if he could rent part of her home to use as a boarding school. Magdelaine agreed and quickly set up a classroom and living quarters for twelve Metis and Indian children. Although she was Catholic, she was tolerant of the Reverend's additional interest in converting the children to Protestantism, as she recognized the value of the education he offered them.

Magdelaine's mastery of reading and writing in French and English seems linked to having the school in her home. Perhaps she sat in with the young Odawa and Ojibwa students and picked up the skills she had lacked for so long. Once literate, Magdelaine became a teacher herself, enthusiastically sharing Catholic cate-chism with any children who appeared on her doorstep. Some of the students educated in her home grew up to be teachers on the island. Though it never had a formal name, Magdelaine's school helped many young people learn how to deal with Americans and their institutions.

Magdelaine was a profoundly religious woman. Her charity extended beyond her involvement with the school to the island's poor, some of whom survived the long, harsh winters because of her compassionate aid. In the 1820s, Magdelaine donated the land beside her home for a new St. Anne's Church. With the new church came a resident priest, which the island hadn't had since 1765. His name was Father Samuel Mazzuchelli, and he stayed in Magdelaine's home until he settled into his own. Soon Father Mazzuchelli and Magdelaine had opened a school for Catholic children.

Magdelaine became known for her warm and gracious hospitality. Her home was open to any and all visitors. She stayed in touch with the changing world of wilderness trade and her friends in the fur trade. Her influence in that world was still powerful, whether she used it on behalf of old friends or newcomers.

Visitors wishing to understand the spirit and history of the Mackinac Island area found in Magdelaine the perfect guide. She not only taught them about it with words, she embodied it. Alexis de Tocqueville, a French writer who traveled through North America

Madame LaFramboise's house on Mackinac Island.
Photo taken after her death, probably in the 1870s.
—Don Gentner. Courtesy Judith Stewart

and wrote a book about his experiences, visited around 1831. An account from the time describes how his face glowed with pleasure as he conversed with Magdelaine in French about her Odawa heritage. Literary critic and editor Margaret Fuller was another guest. In her book *Summer on the Lakes, in 1843*, Fuller wrote,

> The house where we lived belonged to the widow of a French trader, an Indian by birth, and wearing the dress of her country. She spoke French fluently and was very ladylike in her manners. She is a great character among them. They were all the time coming to pay her homage, or to get her aid and advice, for she is, I am told, a shrewd woman of business.

Henry Schoolcraft, an Indian agent for the government who studied the geography and peoples of the area, also visited Magdelaine. Schoolcraft's research and journals about Indian life and legends served as important source material for Henry Wadsworth Longfellow's epic poem, "The Song of Hiawatha."

During negotiation of the second Chicago Treaty of 1832–1833, Magdelaine took a firm stand with white lawmakers. An earlier treaty in 1817 had taken much fertile agricultural land in southern and western Michigan away from the Odawa, yet white farmers and settlers wanted more. In 1833, for a small payment, the Odawa ceded the last parcel of their land, giving the United States total possession of Michigan's lower peninsula south of the Grand River. By talking with the right men and using her skill at diplomacy, however, Magdelaine helped ensure that Catholic Indians along the shores of the Great Lakes could remain in their camps and villages.

Magdelaine LaFramboise had the money and social standing to surround herself with nineteenth-century luxury. Instead, she stayed true to her roots, never remarried, and lived a simple life. When she died in 1846, she was buried at the foot of the altar in the church she had helped establish. (Her remains were later moved into the cemetery when a new church was built.) The big home on Huron Street, which serves as an inn today, still stands, a reminder of a woman who enriched every community to which she belonged.

Left, *poet Elizabeth Chandler;* right, *Laura Haviland, with slavers' equipment* —State Archives of Michigan

Elizabeth Chandler and Laura Haviland

UNITED AGAINST SLAVERY

FROM BABYHOOD ONWARD, Elizabeth Margaret Chandler knew the feeling of loss. Her mother died two days after Elizabeth's birth in 1807, and her father passed away when she was only eight years old. But, raised by relatives, she grew up surrounded by love. These two experiences, equally powerful, may account for the sensitivity and talent Elizabeth showed for poetry. When she was a teenager, her poems began to win her national recognition. In particular, she used her pen to wage war on slavery.

After Elizabeth's mother died, her maternal grandmother and namesake, Elizabeth Evans, came to the Chandlers' farm in Delaware to take care of Elizabeth and her brothers, William, who was three, and Thomas, a toddler. Soon Grandmother Evans took the children home with her to Philadelphia. There, their mother's sisters Jane, Ruth, and Amelia also stepped in to help raise the children. All three aunts belonged to the Society of Friends, or Quakers. A Christian sect, the Quakers believed in the direct relationship of every human being with God. They sought to live in truth and sincerity, emphasizing humanity's goodness while working to eliminate its evils. Quakers shunned luxury, spoke and dressed plainly, and were exceptionally courteous. The Society of Friends got the name "Quakers" because of the shaking movements some made in prayer.

The quartet of charitable, concerned Evans women lovingly raised Elizabeth and her brothers. When Elizabeth was old enough, her aunts enrolled her in the local Friends' church school. She wrote her first poem at age nine, the year after her father died.

Reflections on a Thundergust
When lightnings flash, and thunders roll,
To God I will direct my soul,
When sorrows assail my troubled mind
In God I can my refuge find,
Preserved by Him in every snare
I'll join Him in heaven with angels there.

At school, Elizabeth learned about the misery of African slaves in America, and seeds of a lifelong concern were planted. Since its founding, the United States had been deeply divided about slavery. By the early 1800s, the number of slaves in the country approached four million. Vulnerable to all kinds of abuse, slaves were often beaten, their families were broken up, and they were denied education and freedom. At first, slavery had flourished in both the North and the South. But in the North, abolitionists, who opposed slavery, succeeded in getting it outlawed. Next, they turned their attention to the South. Quakers opposed slavery as a sin against human rights, and many spoke out against it to the U.S. Congress.

Elizabeth's formal education ended when she was thirteen, but she continued studying on her own. She especially loved literature and poetry, and she tirelessly composed poems. At sixteen, she had an appealing oval face and graceful, arching eyebrows. Her large, dark eyes expressed both compassion and a lively interest in the world. She heaped her thick, dark hair high and wore elegant yet simple clothes, often gray or beige, since Quakers did not wear bright colors. Describing Elizabeth, her friend and mentor Benjamin Lundy would later say, "Her faculties were bright and vigorous—her perceptions quick and penetrating."

Elizabeth entered and won some poetry contests, and was even able to sell some of her essays and verses about the beauties of nature. Meanwhile, America's controversial practice of slavery moved into the center of public debate. Lundy, a Quaker like Elizabeth, joined the debate by publishing a weekly antislavery newspaper, the *Genius.* In 1826, when Elizabeth was eighteen, Lundy saw her poem "The Slave-ship." It begins:

> The Slave-ship was winding her course o'er
>   the ocean,
> The winds and the waters had sunk unto rest;
> All hush'd was the whirl of the tempest's commotion
> That late had awaken'd the sailor's devotion,
> When terror had kindled remorse in his breast.
> And onward she rode, though by curses attended,
> Though heavy with guilt was the freight that
>   she bore,
> Though with shrieks of despair was the midnight
>   air rended,
> And ceaseless the groans of the wretches ascended,
> That from friends and from country forever she tore.

In the poem, a noble African chief, now a captive, throws himself overboard rather than become "the conqueror's spoil." Elizabeth was disappointed when "The Slave-ship" won only third place in a competition. Then she got a letter from Lundy; he wanted to reprint it in his newspaper. Lundy went on to suggest that Elizabeth contribute essays and poems to his newspaper on a regular basis. We can only imagine her elation. She would write for the *Genius* for the next three years.

Early nineteenth-century America expected women to be homebodies without opinions. As a Quaker, however, Elizabeth had been taught to form opinions. Fortunately, in addition to her antislavery writings, Lundy welcomed her articles about equal education for women, the fate of handicapped people, the treatment of Native Americans, and the horrors of war.

In 1827, when Elizabeth was twenty, beloved Grandmother Evans died. Elizabeth and her brother Thomas went to live with their Aunt Ruth. By this time, Elizabeth had come to care about abolition more than any other cause. But within the Quaker religion, she faced a dilemma. Some abolition work required citizens to break laws—for example, helping runaway slaves. Traditional Quakers believed that slavery was an evil that should be ended, but they also believed that no federal laws should be broken in the effort. Slavery would come to an end, they believed, in God's own time.

However, other Quakers felt called to stronger action against slavery, Elizabeth included. She decided to leave the church of her childhood and join a break-off group of Quakers known as Hicksites. Led by Quaker minister Elias Hicks, the Hicksites stressed the importance of the individual's conscience and private relationship with God. Also more liberal in culture and dress, Hicksites believed in education for free blacks and in buying "free produce"—that is, buying only those goods not generated by slave labor. Elizabeth wrote essays for the Hicksite journal even as she mailed poems and articles off to Lundy. In 1829, Lundy asked Elizabeth if she would be the editor of a special women's portion of the *Genius*. She gladly accepted.

But a big change was waiting in the wings. Ever since Grandmother Evans died, Elizabeth's brother Thomas, now twenty-five, had thought of moving west. In 1830, he, Aunt Ruth, and Elizabeth made plans to emigrate. Thomas bought land in Lenawee County, Michigan Territory. It lay sixty miles southwest of Detroit, within a small, newly settled community named Logan and near the village of Tecumseh. Elizabeth could have stayed in the east, where she had already gained fame as a poet, journalist, and abolitionist. Instead, she chose to pioneer.

In June of 1830, Thomas went into training with a local farmer. He would need skills to survive in the new land. Two months later, with Ruth, Thomas, and a young servant girl, Emily Johnston, Elizabeth left her Philadelphia home, never to see it again. She was twenty-three years old. The little party floated west on the Erie Canal, then crossed Lake Erie on a sailing ship. After the crossing, during her one comfortable night in Detroit, Elizabeth wrote a friend that the memory of the boat's motion "interfered sadly with my rest and dreams."

They left Detroit early the next morning in a carriage. Bumping along log or "corduroy" roads, they were "battered . . . in a most ungentle manner, but at least with undamaged bones," Elizabeth wrote. When they reached Lenawee County, they had the breathtaking sight of their new land and the tiny village of Logan in Raisin Township, named for the nearby Raisin River.

At first they stayed with the Comstock family. Darius Comstock or "Uncle Darius," a kind, helpful Quaker and abolitionist, had built a sawmill on the Raisin River. Thomas's property lay next to the Comstocks' on "a rising piece of land" that Elizabeth named "Hazel-bank." Soon they had a large cabin, one and a half stories high, built of white oak logs. Ruth and Elizabeth helped fit the glass into its six windows. They moved in on November 2. A few months later, Elizabeth wrote her Aunt Jane, "It gives me great pleasure to inform thee that I am quite contented and happy."

The new arrivals settled in. Thomas worked hard at farming and brought in harvests of grain and hay. Elizabeth and Ruth planted fruit trees and a garden with vegetables and flowers. They made candles, raised chickens and hogs, and learned how to spin wool. Emily took care of the household chores. For diversion, the women went out to pick wild plums or had quilting parties. Mail came once a week, while their letters took about two weeks to reach Philadelphia. Elizabeth taught Emily to read and write. The whole family took pleasure in Elizabeth's pet cat, which knew how to unlatch the cabin door by itself. Every now and then, for a special occasion, Thomas borrowed a horse and wagon and they went for a visit to the larger town of Adrian.

Meanwhile, Raisin grew as a Quaker settlement. It and other nearby settlements didn't lack for marriageable men. But, as Elizabeth wrote her aunts, "There is a much larger circle, particularly of females, who seem to maintain the majority with us . . . . I still keep true in allegiance to the single sisterhood." Quakers regarded marriage differently from most Americans at that time. Women who didn't marry had a respected place in the Society of Friends.

Elizabeth continued to write for Lundy. In addition, Lundy told her, twenty or more other newspapers were copying and highly praising her essays and poems. Some of her writings were set to music and sung at Quaker gatherings, especially among abolitionist Friends. Elizabeth was still an ardent abolitionist herself. In October 1832, she wrote to a friend, "We have succeeded in establishing an association here, which we call 'The Logan Friends Anti-Slavery Society.' Our members are as yet few, but an interest in the subject appears to increase throughout the neighborhood, and if we can keep it 'afloat,' I hope it may, in time, be a means of usefulness."

A neighbor, Laura Smith Haviland, shared Elizabeth's passion for the emancipation of slaves. Laura and her husband, Charles, attended the Anti-Slavery Society gatherings with Elizabeth in the meetinghouse. Gradually, more and more neighbors joined as well. Elizabeth used words to fight slavery, influencing the nation with her poems and essays and spurring people to action. Laura, a year younger than Elizabeth, recruited and organized anyone who believed slavery was wrong and should be abolished. Those who listened to Elizabeth and Laura in the little wood meetinghouse heard the newborn heartbeat of resistance in Michigan Territory.

But Elizabeth's contributions were soon cut short. In the spring of 1834, not long after neighbors helped raise the Chandlers' barn, Elizabeth fell ill with intermittent fever and chills. She was bedridden throughout the summer, often too ill to sit up. At that time, malaria plagued the United States even as far north as Michigan. Elizabeth may have had malaria or perhaps cholera. In spite of the doctor's efforts, she declined. Ruth wrote to her sister Jane that Elizabeth was "perfectly calm and reconciled" during the long, wretched sickness.

On November 2, 1834, exactly four years after she and her family joyously moved into their new house, Elizabeth died. Her coffin was set into a woodland burial ground near Hazel-bank, in keeping with her wishes.

The Silver Glade

Lay me not, when I die, in the place of the dead,
With the dwellings of man round my resting place spread
But amidst the still forest, unseen and alone,
When the waters go by with a murmuring tone;
Where the wild bird above me may move its dark wing,
And the flowers I have loved from my ashes may spring.

After her death, collections of Elizabeth's writings sold thousands of copies. The profits went to antislavery groups. Two years after Elizabeth's death, the number of antislavery groups in Lenawee County had risen to fifteen. Darius Comstock chaired a state conference of these societies, which merged to become the Michigan Anti-Slavery Society. Thomas Chandler helped write the new society's constitution. What Elizabeth had helped to establish, her family, along with the Havilands and the Michigan Society of Friends, would carry on.

Elizabeth's friend Laura Haviland had moved to Raisin a year before the Chandlers. The two women had only four years of friendship and antislavery work together before Elizabeth died, but Laura would continue the work long after.

Laura had always had a strong personal feeling about how she should serve God. Laura Smith was born in 1808 in Ontario, Canada. Her mother, Sene Blancher, was from Vermont, and her father, Daniel Smith, had been born in eastern New York. In 1815, when Laura was seven, they moved to a remote village in New York. There were no schools, so Laura's mother educated her. She read every book she could get her hands on, including one on the slave trade by John Woolman. "I became deeply interested in [the] . . . history . . . of the capture and cruel middle passage of negroes, and of the thousands who died on their voyage and were thrown into the sea to be devoured by sharks that followed the slave ships . . . ." She felt great compassion for the kidnapped Africans.

In November 1825 Laura Smith, seventeen years old, married Charles Haviland. The parents of both were ministers in the Society of Friends. Like Elizabeth Chandler, Laura and Charles resigned from the traditional, orthodox Society of Friends to work more effectively, they believed, against slavery. They joined the Wesleyan Methodist Church, and Laura became a minister.

Fours years later, Charles and Laura moved to Michigan Territory. They built a cabin in Raisin Township, prepared farmland, and returned to the Quaker faith. They had just gotten settled when the Chandlers arrived.

After Elizabeth died, Laura and Charles's first venture into social reform was to establish a school in their home for nine "poorhouse" children. Poorhouses were homes for the poor and homeless. Laura did not discriminate; both girls and boys, of any color, were welcome. The Raisin Institute, as it was called, began in 1837, the year Michigan became a state. Children learned writing, reading, and arithmetic as well as religion, sewing, and farming. The idea was to give children job skills so that they could break the cycle of poverty. Despite difficult financial times, the institute miraculously evolved.

By 1845, Laura was thirty-seven and had borne seven children. That year rheumatic fever struck her family. Rheumatic fever spreads quickly, causing pain and swelling in the joints and heart. The fever took Laura's husband, her youngest child, and her parents. It almost killed Laura, too. In addition to the grief of this loss, Laura found herself homeless due to taxes and debt, with six young children to feed. Friends took the broken, penniless family in, and Laura ultimately paid off her obligations. She would struggle financially, however, all of her life.

Laura recovered her strength. She tied a bonnet under her chin, threw a shawl around her shoulders, and headed into each day

Illustration of the Raisin Institute, from A Woman's Life Work *by Laura Smith Haviland* —Courtesy Christopher Sirmons Haviland, Havilands.com

with determination. Her older children helped with the smaller ones while Laura ran their farm and the school. In satisfaction and joy, Laura said, "we were surely repaid more than a hundred-fold for all our toiling and heavy burdens borne in founding the Raisin Institute."

The already challenging balancing act of her life didn't stop Laura from the other work she felt called to. In 1846, with other Quakers, Laura began helping runaway slaves get from Cincinnati, Ohio, to Canada. Lenawee County had more than twenty "stations" on the "Underground Railroad," as this important, secret, and illegal route was known. The "stations" were people's homes; black fugitives were hurried into cellars, tunnels, and other hiding places. If slave hunters pursued them, abolitionists signaled each other by ringing church bells or blowing horns. "Passengers" on the railroad traveled by night through rough terrain, with precise directions to the next station. It is estimated that one hundred thousand slaves made this difficult journey to freedom between 1810 and 1850.

An entire black family, the Hamiltons, managed to escape from their Southern owners, the Chesters, and were directed to shelter at Laura's farm. Soon after, a pair of Chester men arrived. Brandishing their pistols, they called Laura a thief and threatened to kill her. Tiny Laura boldly faced them down until local abolitionists arrived and chased the men into the woods. The Chesters put up posters offering a reward of three thousand dollars for Laura's killing. Apparently they didn't like it when she said, "Whatever privilege you claim for yourself, or I claim for myself, I claim for every other human being in the universe, of whatever nation or color."

Laura also traveled to Southern states with supplies for escaping slaves. While there, she collected real equipment used by slave owners and traders: slave binders, neck collars, knee stiffeners, handcuffs, and leg cuffs, all made of heavy, painful iron. Back home, she brought the devices to talks she gave, to make sure that Northern audiences understood the reality of slavery. Other times she asked freed slaves to come and display their deep scars and maimed, crippled bodies.

When the Civil War began in 1861, activity on the Underground Railroad came to a halt. Laura answered President Lincoln's call for nurses. The visits to military hospitals broke her heart. "Every soldier was some mother's son," she said. In 1864, on a visit to distribute supplies in New Orleans, she heard about three thousand Northern prisoners-of-war imprisoned on islands off the coast. Laura actually visited one of the camps to investigate and found starving men in unspeakably filthy quarters. By writing letters and working through her congressmen, she helped gain their release. It was her most impressive Civil War success.

After the war, Laura worked to aid homeless and illiterate blacks. The Freedman's Aid Bureau in Detroit hired her at forty dollars a month—her first salaried job—to collect and distribute supplies to freed slaves. She also fought to improve Michigan's care for poor people of all colors. Later, she wrote, "The county poor houses were but nurseries for prisons." Her efforts helped establish a school and orphanage for boys at Coldwater, Michigan, and one for girls in Adrian.

In her sixties, the woman known by many as "Aunt Laura" took up new crusades. She joined the Woman's Christian Temperance Union to fight against alcohol's effects on American families, and she worked for women's right to vote.

In her seventies, plagued by illness, Laura wrote her autobiography, *A Woman's Life Work.* Sadly, twenty years after the Civil War, blacks fared little better in the North than they had in the South; few Northern whites cared to help them have lives of real freedom. But Laura never flagged in her efforts to collect money and supplies for freed blacks and to start schools for them. Finally, in 1898, at the grand old age of ninety, her labors ceased with her death.

Laura was buried at Birdsall, in the Raisin River valley, beside the Society of Friends church. A statue of her, cast in 1909, stands in front of the courthouse in Adrian, Michigan. Like Elizabeth Chandler, Laura patterned her life after firm beliefs in equality for all, and she never weakened. Both women were pioneers—physically, with the land, but more importantly, morally and spiritually. They helped establish the conscience of their adopted state.

Thine for the oppressed
Laura S. Haviland

Laura Smith Haviland's signature, from her book A Woman's Life Work —Courtesy Christopher Sirmons Haviland, Havilands.com

Emma Edmonds —Michigan Women's Historical Center and Hall of Fame

Emma Edmonds

CIVIL WAR SOLDIER

SARAH EMMA EDMONDSON was born in New Brunswick, Canada, in 1841. As a child, Sarah decided to go by her middle name, Emma, instead. That first taste of choosing her own name must have pleased the girl greatly, because Emma went on to choose many more names during her life, as well as identities to go with them. Later, with a shortened last name, Emma Edmonds became famous as one of the more than four hundred Northern and Southern women who dressed as men and fought in the Civil War. After her time in the army, Emma wrote a book about her adventures.

Emma grew up on a farm. Her father, Isaac, and her mother, Betsie, had four girls and a boy. Emma was the youngest. The boy, Thomas, was disabled, probably by epilepsy, and the girls in the family did much of the farm work. By the time Emma was six, she was working a full day outside with her siblings, planting potatoes in the rocky soil. At age ten, she walked behind a horse, straining to hold plow handles higher than her shoulders. She chopped wood deftly. Ever practical, Emma wore boy's homespun clothes when she worked. She took care of the farm animals, prized the horses, and became an excellent rider. She rode astride, not sidesaddle like most women at that time.

Isaac had an imperious nature. Betsie and her children had to give him instant obedience or harsh discipline—verbal or physical—resulted. Emma wrote later,

> My innate soul was impressed with my mother's wrongs before I ever saw light and I probably drew from her breast with my daily food, any love of independence and my hatred of male tyranny.

Despite her father's abuse, Emma looked back on her childhood as happy. She seemed to have good relationships with her mother and siblings and enjoyed the freedom of growing up on a farm.

According to Betsie, Emma had "healing hands." Early settlers had to perform much of their own doctoring, and as Emma grew up she learned sickroom care and herbal remedies. Once, she was the only one in the family who didn't have a fever. Though she was still a child, she ministered to all the others. When Thomas had one of his frequent losses of consciousness, she responded, staying by his side until he recovered.

When she was about ten, a door-to-door salesman came by and Betsie invited him to dinner. Afterwards, drawn to spirited Emma, he gave her a novel called *Fanny Campbell, the Female Pirate Captain: A Tale of the Revolution.* The book was about a young woman who went to sea disguised as a man. She ended up rescuing her lover from pirates.

Emma cherished the book. She was ecstatic that the character, Fanny, chopped off her curly hair and put on a seaman's uniform. In Emma's opinion, the book had one flaw: the only reason Fanny had done all she did was so that she could marry her sweetheart. She was, Emma wrote later, just "running after a man." But the book gave Emma insight. A woman could run away and pose as a man! Maybe there was a chance for freedom from her father's iron hand.

Emma grew into a slender, attractive girl with dark curly hair. Neighboring farm boys stopped by to visit, but Emma felt no romantic interest. If her gentle mother's harsh life was what lay in store for a wife, she detested the thought of marriage. Instead, Emma dreamed of a life of adventure. But when she was sixteen, she got shocking news. Her father had decided that Emma should marry an older farmer, a friend of his who lived nearby.

In secret, Emma and Betsie talked about what to do. Betsie sympathized with her daughter. After all, she had married Isaac when she was fifteen and had regretted it ever since. They began wedding preparations, but Betsie also wrote to her friend Annie Moffatt, who owned a hat shop in Salisbury, New Brunswick. She asked if Annie would take Emma as an apprentice milliner, or hatmaker.

A reply came quickly: Yes! Emma prepared to leave her family and home. Just in case she needed them, a friend about her age who lived on a neighboring farm, Linus Seeley, gave Emma some of his clothes. One day close to the wedding date, Annie arrived in a carriage while Isaac was off working in the fields. Emma hugged her mother and climbed into Annie's carriage. She would never see her father again.

In Salisbury, Emma had no need for Linus's rough woolen trousers. She bought dresses at a store with the money she earned from making women's hats. She lived in a rented room and made her own friends. Her new experiences gave her tremendous satisfaction. When she was seventeen, she opened a new hat shop in a nearby town with one of her friends, Henrietta Perrigo.

But soon thereafter, Emma vanished. Not even Henrietta knew where Emma went. The abruptness and completeness with which Emma disappeared and the radical change in her life when she reemerged suggest that Emma's father had discovered her whereabouts and perhaps was even on his way to get her.

Emma had moved to the bustling city of St. John, New Brunswick. There, she dressed in a man's suit, shirt, bowtie, and shoes and looked for a job. She found one, selling Bibles door to door. With Emma's change of identity and gender, she assumed a new name: Franklin Thompson. She became an excellent book salesman and publisher's agent and thrived in the unrestricted life of a man earning good commissions. She bought a fine horse and carriage.

In 1859, when she was eighteen, Emma gave in to homesickness and traveled home by stagecoach in her new identity. She knocked on the door and introduced herself as a book salesman—just like the one who had given her that important adventure book years before. Her mother and her sister Frances quickly saw through the disguise and fetched Thomas to join the reunion. Unsure when Isaac might return, Emma explained her disappearance and, this time, bid her family a proper farewell. As she hurried across the farmyard to leave, the animals she had cared for crowded around her. They recognized her!

Emma left Canada in search of opportunity and education. She traveled south and west, ending up in Flint, Michigan. As Franklin Thompson, she sold religious books, lodged at the home of a Methodist pastor, and became close friends with two men: William Morse, a captain in the Second Michigan Volunteer Regiment, and Damon Stewart, a clothing salesman and sergeant in the regiment.

In 1861, two years after Emma's visit home, war was in the air. Seven Southern states had formed a confederacy and seceded from the rest of the country. Southern political leaders had become angry and worried about the direction the country was going. In their eyes, the explosive growth of the industrial North weakened their own position. In addition, the antislavery movement questioned their right to own slaves, four million of whom powered the Southern economy. For several months, President Abraham Lincoln tried to get the states to come back into the Union. That spring, however, Confederate soldiers fired on federal forces and captured Fort Sumter in Charleston, South Carolina. The Civil War began.

President Lincoln called for seventy-five thousand men to join the Northern, or Union, army. Emma, twenty years old, decided to answer his call. She wrote later that the cause of the Union stirred her devotion. Added to this were her "natural fondness for adventure" and the fact that she was "a little ambitious and a good deal romantic." On May 25, 1861, Emma joined the Army of the North—specifically, Company F of the Second Michigan Volunteer Infantry—as Private Franklin Thompson. Army physical examinations were cursory, and with the outbreak of war, most healthy-looking males were accepted. Emma joined up as an army nurse. The majority of army nurses at that time were male.

First she went through basic training: twelve days, nine hours a day, of drilling and handling firearms at the Detroit fairgrounds. Farm life had prepared her for the intense physical workout and discipline. After training, her regiment boarded the train for Washington, D.C. Damon Stewart was already there and welcomed Frank into his tent. Later he said that he never once suspected that his friend was a woman, though everyone made fun of Frank's "ridiculous little boots."

How did Emma and other female Civil War soldiers manage to hide their identity? Soldiers slept in their clothing, didn't change clothes often, and bathed in rivers and ponds. Emma would slip out after dark to bathe. Personal modesty was also greater at that time, even among the same sex. Women weren't the only ones who may have avoided the crude toilets—long trenches sided by a pole fence—and headed for the woods instead. Or they waited until the toilets were vacant or underused. The women must have had other tricks that are unrecorded, which we will never know.

Thousands of volunteers had streamed into Washington, and white tents sprang up like mushrooms in every open space. Contagious disease spread easily in crowded and unsanitary conditions, and temporary hospitals soon formed in churches, schools, hotels, and private mansions. Emma nursed the ill, drilled, worked on road construction, and took her turn standing guard. She also made friends in the regiment, chief among them army chaplain James Butler and his wife, Kate, a nurse.

In July 1861, the Union Army readied for an attack on the Confederate Army. They had received orders to march about twenty-five miles to Bull Run, an area in Virginia with a stream by that name. "Oh, what excitement and enthusiasm that order produced," Emma remembered. As an army nurse, she would accompany the troops.

The Union Army was sure of winning. Maybe the Confederates would even surrender and the war would be over. That Sunday morning, local citizens, congressmen, and other public officials rode alongside the troops in their carriages. They brought their families and picnic baskets and were ready to watch the Confederates get trounced.

But Confederate forces were waiting. Soon Emma and the Butlers found themselves in a hell of "confusion, destruction and death." The earth grew stained and slippery with blood. The three carried water to the troops and tended to the wounded and dying. The Union soldiers retreated, hindered by hysterical onlookers.

Back in Washington, D.C., Emma and the Butlers continued to nurse maimed soldiers and those with measles, intestinal disease, and severely contagious typhoid fever. They survived several other horrifying battles in the following months, but on the whole, the rest of the year was a standoff between the two sides.

In 1862 the standoff shifted. That spring, seventy thousand new Union soldiers arrived at Fort Monroe, near Yorktown, Virginia, to prepare for a march on Richmond, Virginia, the capital of the Confederacy. Emma worked at a tent hospital near the fort. She also served as postman, riding twenty-five miles and back between Camp Scott and Fort Monroe to get the mail. Another post rider on the route had been killed by "bushwhackers" who stole the mail, but that didn't stop Emma. Neither did a fall she took while riding, which resulted in multiple serious injuries. Refusing a doctor's examination, Emma healed herself.

At Yorktown, Emma fell in love with a young lieutenant, James Vesey, whom she had known in the past. But tragically, Vesey was killed by a sniper. Emma couldn't bear the grief alone. She found her friend Kate and poured out her story—not just her love for James, but also, her true identity. Astounded, Kate comforted her and swore to keep Emma's secret, even from her husband.

Around this time, James Butler approached Emma with the possibility of greater adventure than she had dreamed of. Recently, a Union spy had been seized and hanged. Would she have the courage to replace him? After a tentative yes, she traveled to Washington, where generals and other military men interviewed her. They approved her for the job.

Back at Fort Monroe, Emma got her first assignment. Across a line nearby, thousands of Confederate soldiers were preparing to keep the Northerners from advancing. Union generals wanted to know more about their defenses. Kate Butler helped Emma darken

Emma Edmonds as Private Frank Thompson. Original illustration from her book, Nurse and Spy in the Union Army *(1865)*
—Bentley Historical Library, University of Michigan

her skin and dress as a black slave, then Emma crossed the Confederate line at night. The next day, she fell in with a group of slaves moving gravel in a construction site. By nightfall Emma's hands were covered with blisters. The next morning, she took water to Confederate soldiers and listened to conversations. She memorized types of mounted guns, drew a diagram of fortifications, and uncovered the identity of a Confederate spy. On the third night, while taking dinner to guards on the outer edge of the camp, Emma faded into the darkness and ran back to Fort Monroe. Even the general leading the troops, George McClellan, praised the daring of Frank Thompson and shook the young man's hand.

Emma claimed about eleven spy missions in all during her time as a soldier. Once she masqueraded as an Irishwoman; another time as a female slave. In Louisville, Kentucky, introduced into society as fashionable rebel sympathizer Charles Mayberry, she flushed out two Confederate informers. Some historians question whether this part of Emma's story is true. While she might have embellished some facts, it makes sense that Emma would be attracted to spy missions and succeed at them. She was already good at leading a double life.

In May, the Union army began its march on Richmond. Emma's regiment clashed with Confederate troops at the Battle of Williamsburg. During the battle, Emma's friend William Morse had his leg shattered, and she rushed to carry him out of further danger. He would live to see Emma again, years later. Her friend Damon Stewart was also injured. One fifth of the soldiers in Emma's regiment were killed in the battle. Emma wrote,

> Oh war, cruel war! . . . How many joyous and bright prospects thou hast blasted; and how many hearts and homes have thou made desolate. As we think of the great wave of woe and misery surging over the land, we cry out in very bitterness of soul—Oh, God! How long, how long?

Emma also lived through the terrible Battle of Antietam in Maryland in the fall of 1862. Dodging cannon balls and rifle shots, she ran to tend the wounded. One, she discovered, was a young woman dressed in uniform like herself. The soldier died as Emma knelt close beside her. Surely Emma wondered if that would be her own fate. Union troops turned back to Washington to rest. Ultimately, they gave up on Richmond.

Emma passed a miserable, muddy winter with General Ulysses Grant's troops near the Confederate stronghold of Vicksburg, Mississippi. There was hardly any food. The year of 1862 ended in disastrous defeat for the Union in battles around Fredericksburg, Virginia, against General Robert E. Lee. Emma was injured while bandaging a wounded officer during a raging fight. Her horse, named Rebel, panicked at some noise and kicked her with such force that she flew through the air. She scrambled to her feet, led the horse to safety, fashioned a sling for her shredded, useless arm, and returned to tend to the injured.

By the end of 1862, it was evident that Emma was fighting more than the war. Severe bouts of fever and chills told her that she had the deadly mosquito-borne disease, malaria. This time, she knew, she wouldn't survive without serious medical attention. She decided she had to leave the army.

> I never for a moment considered myself a deserter. I left because I could hold out no longer, and to remain and become a helpless patient in a hospital was sure discovery, which to me was far worse than death.

After recovering from one of her bouts of fever, Emma left her regiment on April 22, 1863, for Washington, D.C. There, as a woman under her own identity, she rested and recovered, still working as a nurse.

While she got better, she decided to pursue her old dream of education. Emma went to Oberlin, Ohio, where, in men's clothing, she took some courses at Oberlin College. By now, however, her enthusiasm for her male identity seems to have begun to fade. At one point, she checked out of her boardinghouse, went to Pittsburgh, Pennsylvania, threw away her male wardrobe, and returned to Oberlin. She reregistered at the same boardinghouse as Emma Edmonds. No one recognized her.

In Oberlin, she wrote her memoir, *Unsexed; or, The Female Soldier, also known as Memoirs of a Soldier, Nurse and Spy*. It quickly became a bestseller; eventually 175,000 copies were sold. Emma donated every penny of her profits to agencies for war veterans. Soon she went back to nursing, journeying restlessly from hospital to hospital, wherever she was needed the most.

In the fall of 1864, while living and working in Harpers Ferry, West Virginia, Emma happened upon Linus Seeley, the young neighbor who had helped her escape so long ago. A widower, he worked as a carpenter there. After the war ended in April 1865, Emma returned to Oberlin College, and Linus followed. Two years later, they married. With her fondness for name changes, Emma had to put her stamp on her new one. She switched the final two letters of Linus's last name to make "Seelye."

Emma bore three children. Sadly, all of them died young. Emma and Linus ran an orphanage in Oberlin and, later, one for black children in Louisiana. They lived in other states, as well. Emma's malaria still plagued her, but in 1883, when she was forty-two, she and Linus adopted two boys.

Friends persuaded Emma to seek a veteran's pension—regular money from the government in recognition of soldiers' service. To do so, she traveled back to Flint, Michigan. There she looked up her old friend, Damon Stewart, who was thunderstruck when the plump, middle-aged woman at his door told him she was Frank Thompson. William Morse was no less shocked. The three talked with pleasure about army days. Damon told other comrades in Company F about Emma, and she was able to get confirmation from all of them in writing that she had, indeed, served as a soldier and nurse and deserved a pension.

There was desertion on her record, though. Thanks to her old comrades' influence, the War Department in Washington agreed to review her case. After some debate, in 1884 Congress granted her an honorable discharge. Desertion charges were erased, and Emma was awarded a pension of twelve dollars a month.

When the Seelyes' son Frederick married in 1891 in Texas, Emma and Linus moved south to LaPorte to join the newlyweds. In Texas, fondly remembering General McClellan, Emma became the only female member of the George B. McClellan veterans' post.

Seven years later, in 1898, Emma died. She was only fifty-seven; malaria probably shortened her life. First buried in LaPorte, she was moved at the insistence of her fellow veterans to the Washington Cemetery in Houston. Her grave marker reads "Emma E. Seelye, Army Nurse."

Lucy Thurman —Michigan Women's Historical Center and Hall of Fame

5

Lucy Thurman

TRUE TO HER RACE

ON A SPRING DAY IN 1882, about thirty people gathered at a meeting of the Woman's Christian Temperance Union, a group dedicated to improving the health and well-being of families across the United States. Standing before the mostly white audience, a handsome, dignified African American woman began to speak. Her voice was pleasing to the ear, and her dynamic personality soon became apparent. The crowd sat mesmerized. Without a script or notes, and with confidence and conviction, the woman spoke words of power and eloquence. This woman was Lucy Thurman, one of the great social activists of her day. When Lucy spoke, people didn't just listen. They were also inspired and compelled to take action.

Lucy was born in Canada in 1849. Her mother was Katherine Campbell, some of whose ancestors had come to Canada from Haiti. Katherine married Nehemiah Henry Smith in Oshawa, Ontario. The marriage was typical for that time: the bride was thirteen, and the groom, thirty-four. Katherine went on to have three daughters and three sons. Lucinda, or Lucy, was a "middle child" in order of birth. Records of her childhood and schooling are scant, showing only that she finished elementary school. After that, if she didn't attend a formal school, it's likely her parents taught Lucy at home.

In whatever way they taught, formally or informally, the Smith parents must have done a good job. Lucy wasn't the only sibling who went on to become a leader. Her brother, Charles Spencer Smith, went to college in the United States and became an African Methodist Episcopal minister, and even a bishop. Called "one of the most profound thinkers the race has ever produced," he was long remembered for his inspiring lectures.

Living in Canada, Lucy and her family weren't faced with the personal specter of slavery endured by black people in the United States. However, Canada was a major destination for runaway Southern slaves. Through the Smiths' church and community, the family must have gained firsthand knowledge of the evils of

W. Wells Brown,

Lucy's mentors Frederick Douglass (left), *probably around 1885–1890, and William Wells Brown* (right).
—Douglass photo by Pullman; courtesy Frederick Douglass National Historic Site, Washington, D.C. FRDO 3932. Wells Brown photo, courtesy Division of Rare and Manuscript Collections, Cornell University Library

slavery. Perhaps this exposure to the plight of American blacks moved Lucy to make a difference. Or she may have had other motivations and influences, such as her parents' teaching. However it occurred, by the time Lucy reached young adulthood she was dedicated to improving the lives of "people of color," as she called her race.

By 1866, the year after the end of the American Civil War, Lucy had made her way to Rochester, New York. There she met the renowned black abolitionists Frederick Douglass and Dr. William Wells Brown. Before the war, the two men had worked tirelessly and effectively against slavery. Now, the freed American slaves floundered, homeless, in disarray and extreme poverty. At age seventeen, Lucy felt their plight deeply. She wanted to be part of their new lives.

Douglass and Brown helped Lucy find a teaching position in Maryland. In her free time, she helped Douglass and other black leaders in their work and gained valuable leadership skills and experience along the way. An extensive antislavery network and movement of both black and white people had evolved before the war. Now the same network was recruiting ardent, social-minded individuals to help reconstruct battered post-war America.

Before the war, Douglass's brilliant, persuasive public speaking had done much to convey the horrors of slavery to the American public. The son of a slave, Douglass had managed to educate himself before escaping from slavery in Maryland at age twenty-one. In speeches, he reminded audiences that he wore his real diploma on his back, referring to deep scarring there from a horsewhip. Frederick Douglass was the name he chose for himself after he was free.

Later Douglass founded an abolitionist newspaper, *North Star,* which he edited until 1860. After the Civil War, the federal government hired him for a number of jobs. He ran a bank for freed slaves and served as a diplomat in the Caribbean and as a U.S. marshal. He continued touring the country and speaking. As a spokesman for freed slaves, he helped them survive.

William Wells Brown became another of the abolition movement's most gifted orators. He had been born a slave in Kentucky, and after escaping in the 1830s, he fought slavery through speeches and writings. In 1853, he published a novel, *Clotel,* about slave daughters of Thomas Jefferson. It was the first novel by an African American.

After three years, Lucy left her teaching job, moved to Jackson, Michigan, got married, and started a family. By now she was twenty-one. Her husband, Henry William Simpson, was a church minister, and they had two boys, John and William.

As Mrs. Lucy Simpson, she jumped headlong into social reform for black people. Many progressive women were focusing on alcohol as a destructive force in society. Families were being broken and impoverished by husbands with a drinking problem, they said, and at that time, wives had few rights over their children or their finances. If husbands endangered their families, wives could do little about it. The temperance movement—the movement to limit or ban alcohol—wasn't just about drinking. It was mainly about improved conditions for families. In some instances it was also tied to women's rights—in particular, the right to vote. These were the outstanding reforms women believed to be crucial in the 1870s.

In 1873, when she was twenty-four, Lucy attended a women's temperance crusade, or gathering, in Toledo, Ohio. Women in Ohio were some of the most active in social reform; the following year, the Woman's Christian Temperance Union (WCTU) was founded in Cleveland. At the crusade, stepping confidently up on the platform with a baby in her arms, Lucy pleaded with eloquence for society "to provide work for people of color."

Lucy joined the WCTU as its only black founding member. She believed in the organization's goals: better human health, jobs for the poor, help for assorted social problems, and especially, assistance for victims of alcohol abuse. Most of the women in the temperance movement and the WCTU were white, but Lucy didn't let that stop her. Perhaps she recognized how effective and powerful the organization could be in bettering society—black families included.

Lucy's natural gift for public speaking had been honed during her apprenticeship with the Rochester abolitionists. Now she became one of the WCTU's most sought-after speakers. Traveling through Michigan, Indiana, and Illinois, she gave lectures to audience after audience. As she traveled, her hands kept busy creating lovely crocheted items and pieced quilts.

Sometime during the next years, Lucy's first marriage ended, probably due to her husband's death. In 1883, when she was thirty-four, she married Frank Thurman, a widower and barbershop owner in Jackson, Michigan. Like Lucy, Frank had grown up in Canada, but he had been born in Indiana. Fearful that their baby might be stolen into slavery in the South, his parents had sent their young son to safety in Ontario, where an uncle raised him.

Frank brought two daughters to his marriage with Lucy, and the couple had two more children together. His profession gave them a respectable and prosperous lifestyle. Their children received good educations. Their son Frank went on to medical college, and their daughter Gladys went to the University of Michigan. Tragically, Gladys died there, from an infectious disease.

Lucy and Frank were one in their desire to work for equal rights and education for African Americans. In Jackson, they became known for their warmth, openness, and charity toward less fortunate people of color. They worked on many humanitarian projects, and their membership in the American Methodist Episcopal Church brought them strength and comfort. Their home was a gracious gathering place for their many friends, including Frederick Douglass, whose mane of hair had become quite white, but whose dark eyes were no less determined. Black educator Booker T. Washington and his wife were also guests there.

In 1893, Lucy became WCTU's first black Superintendent of Temperance Work among Colored People. This enabled her to concentrate her efforts on organizing among women of her own race. To do so, Lucy traveled as far as California and into every southern state. In the South, she focused on schools, where she talked about education and abstaining from liquor as a means to a decent life. She visited tiny towns, and even though she was a Northerner, Southern blacks felt she understood the problems they faced. They remembered her speeches for years. In 1897, on a trip through Texas, she organized fifteen WCTU chapters, also known as unions. The state-level WCTU chapter of black women called itself the Thurman Union after her.

The WCTU's choice of Lucy for superintendent, and its commitment to the work among black women and families, won black women's gratitude and praise. In 1900, at a convention, the Michigan Federation of Colored Women complimented the WCTU, saying, "They have shown the absence of prejudice against us by appointing such women of race as Lucy Thurman and others to positions of trust."

One particularly vital speech Lucy made at a national WCTU convention was called "Work Among Colored People." It was about the huge need for job training and literacy for blacks. Of the four million black people in the United States at the close of the Civil War, she said, barely one-fourth could read. Now, some thirty years later, in southern states with segregated schools, there were about eight million blacks and not even half of them could read. Another plea was for schools and churches to teach abstinence from alcohol.

The WCTU's successes opened Lucy's eyes to the potential created when women organize. She said, "I have always favored the organization of union among the colored women, for it will be to them just what it has been to our white sisters, the greatest training school for the development of women." By "union," she meant a way of organizing in which people work together toward a common cause.

In 1898, Lucy applied this idea in a new way. With her activist friend Elizabeth McCoy, she cofounded the Michigan Association of Colored Women's Clubs and served as its first president. Like its parent organization, the National Association of Colored Women's Clubs (NACWC), the group was dedicated to the welfare, rights, and education of black women and families, as well as the promotion of interracial understanding. With the motto "Lifting as We Climb," the NACWC vowed to show "an ignorant and suspicious world that our aims and interests are identical with those of all good and aspiring women." Traveling around the United States, Lucy met with other women's groups to discuss such topics as educational opportunities and care for the elderly. From 1904 to 1908, she would serve as president on the national level.

In 1896, Lucy sailed across the Atlantic Ocean as a delegate to a WCTU world convention in England. She stayed with a titled English lady who presented her with a silver tea service when she left. The gift has been passed down from generation to generation, and remains in Lucy's family today.

Toward the turn of the century, Lucy spent long hours working to establish the Phyllis Wheatley Home in Detroit, a safe haven for elderly black women. It was named after the African-born woman whom slave traders captured as an eight-year-old child and sold to the Wheatley family in Boston. Phyllis Wheatley began writing poetry at thirteen and gained literary fame. The name would catch on in black communities, and Phyllis Wheatley homes and residences, mostly directed toward young women, would multiply across the country, run either by the National Association of Colored Women or the Young Women's Christian Association (YWCA).

After a lifetime dedicated to improving the lives of black women and families, as well as women and families of all races, Lucy Thurman died on March 29, 1918. She was sixty-nine years old. A multitude of friends attended her funeral, which was arranged by the WCTU. She was buried in Jackson in the Evergreen Cemetery, with a gravestone erected by the Michigan Association of Colored Women's Clubs.

Involved as Lucy had been in honoring Phyllis Wheatley, it was only fitting that, in 1931, the Detroit YWCA named one of its branches after Lucy. The facility was well appointed, with sixty-five rooms, a pool, a gymnasium, a cafeteria, conference rooms, and other amenities. In 1986, when the building was sold and renovated, it became an alcoholism treatment program, a place where people could find help for their disease. Lucy would have been pleased, as this was the problem that first turned her toward a lifetime of activism.

Marguerite deAngeli sketching near Canterbury Cathedral, 1948
—Marguerite deAngeli Collection, Marguerite deAngeli Branch, Lapeer District Library

Marguerite deAngeli

AN ARTFUL LIFE

MARGUERITE LOFFT WAS NOT QUITE TWO when she discovered a pastel portrait that her father, an artist and photographer, had been drawing of a client. The vibrant sticks of colored chalk beckoned to Marguerite. She reached her little hand into the enticing box and, trying each color, made a mark on the canvas. Her father found her and scolded her, but years later she still remembered the thrill of those pastels. "What excitement to feel the soft touch of the canvas and see the bright mark it made," she later wrote of that experience. Already, Marguerite Lofft deAngeli's attraction to the arts was clear. For much of her life she struggled to express the creativity that burgeoned inside her, and she succeeded—as a musician, as a visual artist, and most notably, as an author of children's books.

Marguerite Lofft was born in Lapeer, Michigan, on March 14, 1889. Her sister, Nina, was fifteen months older, and they would eventually have four brothers: Arthur, Harry, Walter, and Dick. Her father, Shadrach, had a sunny disposition. Her mother, Ruby, was a homemaker and excellent cook who sewed exquisite clothing for her family. Both parents encouraged their children to pursue whatever special abilities they had.

With many relatives in Lapeer, Marguerite had a childhood full of gatherings and celebrations and summer picnics at Lake Nepessing. She and Nina spent most of their time outdoors. Marguerite also loved looking at pictures, reading, and daydreaming. With the minister's wife, she learned to copy watercolors and drawings, but the lack of originality in this practice ultimately frustrated her. She yearned to draw the imaginary figures that danced behind her eyes and to write the stories flowing in her imagination. By the time she was eleven, she was scribbling notes and dialogue on whatever scraps of paper lay about.

In 1902, Marguerite turned thirteen, and her father took a job with the Eastman Kodak Company showing photographers how to use camera film, a new invention. The Loffts moved to a spacious, modern house in Philadelphia, Pennsylvania. Sunday afternoons became a time of enchantment for Marguerite as she spent time in the museum in Memorial Hall, gazing at medieval suits of armor and old carriages, and in the art gallery—which she always saved until last—where the exquisite paintings made her desire to draw and write surge inside her.

Marguerite grew strong, broad-shouldered, and slender. She wore her dark hair fashionably upswept, and her wide-spaced blue eyes looked at the world with curiosity, delight, and humor. When she was fifteen, her parents enrolled Marguerite and Nina in Philadelphia Girls High School. Then a wonderful thing happened. One rainy afternoon at home, Marguerite was singing while Nina accompanied her on the piano. A neighbor heard them and asked Marguerite to sing contralto with a quartet at the Presbyterian church. They would pay her a dollar a week, and she must begin voice lessons immediately. Suddenly interested in nothing but singing, Marguerite left high school and began studying with a teacher, Madame Suelke. Marguerite's wages went toward paying for the lessons.

From that time until she was nineteen, Marguerite sang professionally with church choirs in the area. One choir was in Chester,

Pennsylvania, fourteen miles from home, so each weekend she rode the trolley there for rehearsal Friday evening and stayed to sing in two services on Sunday. She roomed at Mrs. Riley's boarding house, made new friends, and enjoyed dances at Chester Military Academy. Her wages increased to five dollars a week.

When Marguerite was nineteen, while singing in a choir in Overbrook, Pennsylvania, she met a young man of Italian extraction, John Daily deAngeli. A few years older than her, "Dai" (pronounced "Day") played violin in the Philadelphia Symphony Society. Later, Marguerite would write in her autobiography, "He was immediately friendly and I think we knew from that moment that each belonged to the other." Dai often accompanied Marguerite on his violin. He was gentle and good-natured, and Marguerite liked his brown eyes and "rosy" look. They became engaged.

The next year, 1909, Madame Suelke scheduled Marguerite for an audition with the famous Oscar Hammerstein at the Philadelphia

Marguerite deAngeli as a child —Michigan Women's Historical Center and Hall of Fame

Opera House. Hammerstein accepted her as a chorus member and told her that the opera company would soon leave for London on tour. Marguerite could hardly wait to tell her parents! But when she did, they convinced her not to go—and in fact, to give up her singing career. "What about your life with Dai, when you will be away so much?" they asked. In the early 1900s, most parents could not imagine any options for their girls other than being wives and homemakers.

Marguerite went ahead with their simple wedding plans. In April 1910, in the home of a relative in Toronto, Dai and Marguerite were married. Dai then settled into a job selling Edison phonograph records in Canada. All summer, the newlyweds traveled by train, stopping at every town along the route. At night, the sky flashed with the fiery colors of the aurora borealis, the atmospheric phenomenon also known as the northern lights. Marguerite had her first glimpse of the Rocky Mountains, ecstatically describing them in her journal as "a dark wall that went up and up, seemingly forever . . . piercing the blue and taking my heart with it."

From 1911 through 1918, Marguerite was busy as a mother. Son Jack was born in 1911, and the next year another son, Arthur, made them a family of four. Though Marguerite was overwhelmed with domestic duties and child care, the artist within her remained quietly active. While the children were napping, Marguerite found herself studying magazine illustrations. During the summer, she bathed the boys in a tin washtub on a vine-covered back porch, learning anatomy as she washed their backs and observed how their arms and legs moved. And there was still music in her life. Sometimes Dai played his violin and Marguerite accompanied him on the piano. She sang at church and even performed some solo concerts.

In 1913 Marguerite had a daughter, Ruby Catherine, who died five months later of pneumonia. The young family grieved. In 1916, they moved to Detroit. There, Marguerite took drawing and painting lessons and at last found what she had been looking for all her life: a style and way to use color that was completely her own.

With World War I raging, Dai found work in a munitions plant. Marguerite's dear sister Nina contracted tuberculosis, and her health worsened. Marguerite was with her in New Jersey when she took her last breath on April 1, 1918. Wanting to stay close to family, Marguerite asked Dai to move the family back east. They found an apartment directly across from Grandma and Grandpa Lofft, and by fall they were eagerly awaiting the birth of another baby.

However, a deadly flu epidemic was sweeping the country, and Marguerite fell ill. The hospital overflowed with desperately ill and dying people. Nurses themselves lay sick and helpless in emergency wards. Despite moments when she yearned to give up, Marguerite clung to life and pulled through. Miraculously, soon after, a healthy baby girl, Nina, arrived. A month later the war ended.

Three years passed. Through a neighbor, Marguerite met the man who would become her art teacher and mentor, Maurice Bower. An illustrator with Hearst Publications, Maury agreed to work with Marguerite on her art. Dai bought her an easel and charcoal, and she set up in an alcove off the dining room. With Maury's teaching and criticism, Marguerite learned about composition, the power of light and shadow, how to draw the human figure authentically, and much more. For a year, she concentrated on just three drawings. At the end of that year, 1922, Maury declared that the drawings were ready to show to an editor. Marguerite boarded the trolley for New York City—specifically, for the offices of Westminster Press, a religious publisher. The editor bought one drawing to use in a Presbyterian Sunday school paper. Elated, Marguerite visited a Baptist publisher, with the same result. "I was launched," she wrote gleefully.

So began many years of steady work as an artist. Marguerite illustrated for several well-known authors. In the meantime, she had two more sons, Ted in 1925 and Maurice, named after her best friend and mentor, in 1928. When she outgrew her small alcove, her brother Arthur built her a studio above the kitchen. She often used Ted and Maury as models and spent hours in museums and libraries researching illustrations of historical subjects.

The years from 1929 to the onset of World War II in 1941 are burned in the minds and souls of Americans who lived through them. This was the time of the Great Depression. Banks closed, and their clients lost everything. Jobs became scarce. Businesses had few customers since money was scarce. It looked like Marguerite's illustration work might dry up. In 1929, however, Doubleday Publishers contracted her to illustrate a book by a popular children's book writer, Elizabeth Gray Vining, called *Meggy McIntosh.*

Dai soon lost his job and could not find another. The mortgage company took back the house they had lived in for fourteen years, and they had to find another home quickly. With Marguerite's diminishing income as an illustrator, they rented a farm outside Jarrettown, Pennsylvania. Tearfully, they left Nina with her Lofft grandparents to finish high school. Dai and the older boys immediately planted a vegetable garden for food. It was a difficult time. Still, Marguerite wrote, "We had health and each other, the same stories to tell, the same music to lift our hearts, and boundless optimism."

For some time, Marguerite had wanted to write stories as well as illustrate them. Notes and ideas scribbled on scraps of paper cluttered her handbag. Maybe, just maybe, she would illustrate *and* write a story some day. In 1934, a magazine editor she knew, Peggy Lesser, suggested she write a story for six-year-olds. Marguerite pounced on the idea. Within a week, she had written and drawn sketches for the book *Ted and Nina Go to the Grocery Store.* The two main characters were based on her own children. Doubleday bought the book. *Ted and Nina Go to the Grocery Store* was the first American book written for children to read by themselves, without adults.

The American economy in 1934–1935 sank to its worst. Still, there was a market for Marguerite's children's books, which sold for only fifty cents. She quickly wrote and illustrated a second book, *Ted and Nina Have a Happy Rainy Day.* When her friend Peggy Lesser, now an editor at Doubleday, suggested that Marguerite follow these successes with a historical book, her spirits soared. She was on her way to a successful career as an author.

Having spent some of her childhood in Pennsylvania, Marguerite remembered the Amish people, a religious group there known for their simple lifestyle apart from mainstream society. For example, the Amish don't use electricity or drive cars. Marguerite traveled to Lancaster County, Pennsylvania, interviewed Amish people, and dove into their history. The result was *Henner's Lydia*, the first American storybook about a contemporary Amish child. It came out in 1936. A fan wrote Marguerite saying that when he read the book, he sat down and wept, recalling his own boyhood.

Marguerite was an *author!* Royalty checks from her books were helping her family survive. She accepted invitations to talk about her work, in spite of her nervousness about speaking in public. Her parents were proud of Marguerite, finally realizing that by pursuing her personal goals, their daughter was becoming famous.

Soon, ideas for another book were taking shape in Marguerite's imagination. Recalling her father's stories of working in a store in Lapeer when he was young and of the French-Canadian lumberjacks who would come in, Marguerite headed for the Gaspé Peninsula. The Gaspé is a traditional French-Canadian area on the coast of Quebec. Marguerite's parents offered to drive her there, but she declined. She found that people were often more open with their lives if she traveled alone. She went by train and stayed with a local family. She visited the Catholic school and accompanied the family's daughter, a visiting nurse, on her rounds of farmhouse patients. Back home that winter, she pulled *Petite Suzanne* together, the story of a French-Canadian girl and the everyday traditions of her people. It came out in 1937. Soon after, she wrote the third book in her Ted and Nina series, *A Summer Day with Ted and Nina,* published in 1940.

During this period, Marguerite's father died. As a memorial, she began setting down stories he had told her of growing up in Lapeer during the 1870s, as well as some of her own childhood memories. She returned to her birthplace, where relatives drove her around and helped her research the book. There sat her grandma's house, little changed. There was her father's studio window, downtown

A drawing of her children Ted and Nina by
Marguerite deAngeli (undated) —Marguerite deAngeli Collection,
Marguerite deAngeli Branch, Lapeer District Library

over the store. When the book was done, she named it *Copper-Toed Boots*. In the old days, lumberjacks and other laborers wore copper-toed boots to protect their toes. As a boy, her father had yearned for a pair. Some literary experts say *Copper-Toed Boots* is Marguerite's best work.

With Marguerite's earnings, the deAngeli family built a cottage by the ocean at Toms River, New Jersey. The children loved going there, and Marguerite was better able to keep up her steady output of popular books.

One day Marguerite went to Moorestown, Pennsylvania, to speak at the library of the Friends, or Quakers, another religious group known for their belief in simplicity and plainness. During a luncheon in her honor, Marguerite's hosts laughingly told her a story about a spirited little Quaker girl who kicked her plain bonnet down the stairs. Later, Marguerite met the town's beloved ninety-two-year-old, Miss Hannah Carter. Hannah recounted stories from her Quaker childhood. From this experience and further research, Marguerite came up with *Thee, Hannah,* published in 1940.

Several of Marguerite's subsequent books would also feature Amish and Quaker characters. Written with compassion, many of her books were stories of the everyday lives of children outside typical American society. Speaking about one of her later books, Marguerite explained, "To know is to understand." She wrote to dispel fear of the unknown.

In 1941, living in the Philadelphia suburbs near her son Arthur and his wife, Marguerite positioned her drawing table, pencils, paints, and typewriter off one end of the kitchen and began *Elin's Amerika*. This book was about a Swedish girl who immigrated to the colony of New Amsterdam (now New York) with her family in the 1600s. It was published in 1941.

Marguerite and Dai took pleasure in making friends with the many people Marguerite met as she researched her books. Also, they were still making music and sought other musicians to play and sing with. At a musical gathering, they met Ed and Hedwig Ryglewicz. As a boy, Ed had immigrated to the United States from Poland. From his recollections, and with coaching on Polish customs and language, came Marguerite's next book, *Up the Hill,* in 1942. Ed and Hedwig remained lifelong friends of the deAngelis.

In 1944, *Yonie Wondernose* came out, the story of a curious little Amish fellow who finds trouble easily. Marguerite's illustrations for the book won her the prestigious Caldecott Honor Book Award.

For years, Marguerite had had a story tucked away in her head about a biracial girl with one white and one black parent. She had written the book in 1940, but Peggy Lesser, her editor, wasn't sure society was ready for it. Marguerite had two black friends, Nellie

Bright, the principle of a public school, and Jessica Cole, who offered stories of their experiences and advice. *Bright April,* a story about a girl who is "bright and sunny and stormy by turns," was the result. Jessica's daughter became Marguerite's model for the illustrations. Published in 1946, *Bright April* was one of the first books for children to examine racial prejudice in the United States. It won the Lewis Carroll Shelf Award.

By 1947, all five of Marguerite's children had grown up and left home. In her cottage by the ocean, Marguerite began another book, *Jared's Island,* inspired by her surroundings. It was about a Scottish boy who shipwrecked off the coast in the early 1700s. It featured buried treasure and a hidden map.

Ultimately there would be thirteen more books from Marguerite deAngeli's typewriter and drawing board, for a lifetime total of twenty-seven published books. The zenith of her career came in 1950 when she won the Newbery Award for *The Door in the Wall.* The Newbery is the coveted award for the year's most distinguished children's book published in the United States. Set during wartime in thirteenth-century England, *The Door in the Wall* features a young hero who is lame. A disabled friend who played music with the deAngelis had mentioned the need for a book about a child who lives with a handicap.

During the next ten years, Marguerite traveled extensively. When they were in their seventies, Dai and Marguerite finally sold their dear Toms River cottage and moved back to Pennsylvania near their sons. They celebrated their golden anniversary in 1960. Quietly and unpretentiously, Marguerite continued to collect numerous awards and honors for her writing and artwork.

In the summer of 1969, Dai's heart, which had been weak for some time, failed, and he died. For the first time in almost sixty years, Marguerite was without her cherished, supportive partner in music and work. Comforted by her large family, she carried on, continuing to make appearances, give talks, and produce books. And more honors were on their way. On March 14, 1979, on Marguerite's ninetieth birthday, Michigan governor William Milliken declared it Marguerite deAngeli Day. Michigan is just one of the states that claims Marguerite as its own; the other is Pennsylvania. In 1981, a branch of the Lapeer District Library was renamed in her honor.

Marguerite's last book, *Friendship and Other Poems,* came out during her ninety-second year. Six years later, in 1987, Marguerite died of heart failure peacefully in her bed. She was buried in Pennsburg, Pennsylvania. Hers was a lifetime of achievement. She had attained her dream of producing uplifting, encouraging books loved by generations of children.

Left, *Pearl Kendrick;* right, *Grace Eldering*
—Michigan Women's Historical Center and Hall of Fame

Pearl Kendrick and Grace Eldering

SISTERS IN SCIENCE

IN 1932 PEARL KENDRICK, chief of Michigan's medical laboratories in Grand Rapids, shook hands with a new employee, Grace Eldering. Neither woman had an inkling of what lay just ahead: a year of intense vaccine research that would eventually result in millions of lives saved worldwide. It was also the start of an important working partnership and friendship that would endure for nearly fifty years.

Pearl and Grace came from different backgrounds and regions of the country. Pearl was born in Wheaton, Illinois, in 1890. When she was three, her family had moved to New York State. Pearl's father was a Methodist pastor, and the family had moved often as he was transferred from church to church.

After Pearl graduated from high school, she taught school for a while, then went on to get a degree in zoology from Syracuse University. Later, when a reporter asked her why she chose zoology, she said, "I wanted to get this business of evolution settled in my mind." For over half a century already, scholars had been debating evolution, the idea that life-forms modify over generations into different species. The theory of evolution conflicted with the Methodist beliefs Pearl had grown up with, which adhered more closely to the biblical story of creation. Gradually, as Pearl developed into a scientist, she left the creationist theories of her upbringing behind.

For years, Pearl made a career of teaching. Like most rural teachers, she taught many different subjects at various levels. She eventually became the principal of a high school in St. Johnsville, New York. Years later, Grace Eldering, whom Pearl would train in the workplace, described Pearl's skill as a teacher.

> Enthusiasm was probably [her] outstanding characteristic. It pervaded every project she undertook. . . . She was in no way pedantic. She just wanted everyone around her to know all there was to know about a particular subject so that they too, could enjoy her wonder and excitement.

Pearl's fascination with science lay largely untapped during her years as a teacher. Surprisingly, it was war that gave her the opportunity to explore it. In the United States during World War I, with many men away fighting, women stepped into jobs only men had done before—including jobs in the new fields of microbiology and bacteriology, the study of microbes and bacteria. These fields were experiencing a golden age as scientists identified many disease-causing organisms for the first time. Advances in glass-making contributed miraculously powerful new lenses for microscopes. Now, with the war on, women were encouraged to enter these new sciences.

In 1917 at Columbia University in New York City, Pearl enrolled in a course in the study of parasites. She was twenty-seven years old. Later, longing to be part of the scientific community, she took the New York State civil service examination. If she passed, job opportunities would open up for her. How her heart must have soared when she learned she had passed! She accepted a job offer at the state laboratory in Auburn, New York.

Her first assignment was to direct a research group searching for a vaccine for diphtheria. Diphtheria is an infection, mainly in the nose and throat, caused by bacteria. When Pearl began working on it, the disease was all too common in the United States, and about 10 percent of the people who got it died.

Pearl had been in the lab for only a short time, however, when Dr. C. C. Young, a visiting scientist, offered her a job in Michigan. She accepted, and within the year, she moved to Lansing. (Later, Grace Eldering would tease Pearl that she had taken the job because Dr. Young was movie-star handsome.)

In her new job in Lansing, Pearl first worked on a test for the sexually transmitted disease, syphilis. Then, in 1926, Dr. Young moved Pearl to Grand Rapids to set up a new branch laboratory. He promoted her to director of the new branch, as well as associate director of all Michigan laboratories.

"Director" was an impressive title, but when Pearl arrived with her suitcases, what she found was far from impressive. The abandoned building that was to be her lab, on the grounds of what is now the Kent County Community Hospital, had served as an isolation ward for smallpox patients. Workmen had started repairing and remodeling it, but they weren't finished yet. Everything Pearl needed for a working laboratory would have to be gathered from scratch.

In the meantime, part of Pearl's job was to be available, day or night, for emergencies. In cases of diphtheria, for example, fast, accurate diagnosis was critical. A health worker would swab a patient's throat with cotton, then place the bacteria in a sterile glass dish where it was allowed to grow. Health workers could then identify the bacteria under a microscope. In order to be ready to work at any time, Pearl lived in an upstairs apartment in the lab building. While the building was being remodeled, sometimes she had to climb a ladder and crawl through a window to get home. But that didn't bother Pearl. She was "a complete optimist," Grace Eldering wrote later. "Optimism spread around her, as contagious as measles or the common cold."

The state had little money to spend on the laboratory, which meant repairs to the building were minimal. It didn't matter that important work would soon be taking place here—work that would save millions of lives around the world. The floors

71

and walls of Pearl's lab had holes in them. The building seemed about to collapse. But soon, the laboratory was adequately stocked and running. In addition to doing routine tests to diagnose diseases for the Sunshine Hospital (a tuberculosis sanitarium), the city of Grand Rapids, and twenty-eight counties, Pearl and her staff were responsible for the purity of milk and water in western Michigan.

Pearl's hunger for knowledge about her field was not yet satisfied. She made time for courses in pathology, immunology, and research methods at the University of Michigan, and even earned a degree in microbiology.

In 1932, Grace Eldering joined Pearl's staff. Born in 1900, Grace was ten years younger than Pearl. Her mother had immigrated to the United States from Scotland and her father had come from the Netherlands. Grace had grown up in the little town of Rancher, Montana, on the Yellowstone River. After high school, she had entered the University of Montana, but money problems had forced her to drop out after eight semesters.

Grace fell back on one of the few ways a woman could earn money in 1921: she taught school. After four years of saving her wages, Grace was able to return to college and graduate with a degree in biology. She went directly to Hysham, Montana, where she taught high school for a year.

Like Pearl, Grace was very interested in science. "I really wanted to go into medicine," she said later, "but it cost a lot of money." Medical research was a good substitute. Grace had heard that Michigan had outstanding public health laboratories. In addition, the labs had a program in which volunteers could work for no wages for six months while they trained with lab workers for a full-time job. Grace moved to Lansing.

She was accepted as a volunteer and went to work. She had no illusions about her future; after all, a biology major did not exactly qualify as a bacteriologist. She expected to go home to Montana when the training was over and get a hospital job. But after only a few months, an employee in the lab left, opening up an opportunity for Grace. Grace's work had been energetic and wholehearted, and she was offered the job. She said later, "I always knew wherever I went that if a woman worked in a field that was largely occupied by men . . . she had to be a little bit better. I accepted that." It was 1928 and her salary was one hundred dollars a month. It would be thirteen years before she would go back to school and earn a doctorate in bacteriology.

Grace worked in Lansing for several years, then in 1932 she was transferred to Pearl's laboratory in Grand Rapids. Soon after she arrived, the two women decided to study whooping cough, a disease that had killed thousands of children in America, most of them under five years of age. Both Pearl and Grace had had it when they were young. The disease could cause children, especially infants, to cough themselves to death. Complications of the disease often led to weakening, weight loss, and pneumonia. This sickness, also called pertussis, had hit Detroit harder than most areas.

Since the early 1920s, scientists around the world had been working on vaccines to prevent pertussis. Vaccines introduce a safe version of disease-causing organisms into the body, thereby giving it a chance to build defenses, or immunity. After spending a year studying whooping cough, Grace and Pearl wanted to experiment with a vaccine for it. This project would be a big commitment. It was like adding another full-time job—with no extra pay—into their work lives. But the work excited them. They got permission from Dr. Young and went forward.

Pearl, Grace, and their six staff members worked on the vaccine in between their regular duties. As soon as the lab closed in the afternoon, they set out to collect specimens from new patients pointed out to them by doctors. Grace Eldering remembered, "Many of the families we visited were very poor and their living conditions were pitiful. Our watchword became, 'Round to the back and up the stairs.' We listened to sad stories told by desperate fathers who could find no work. We collected specimens by the light of kerosene lamps, from whooping, vomiting, strangling children. We saw what the disease could do."

Creating an effective vaccine means figuring out which ingredients work best and how to prepare them. In addition, Pearl and Grace wanted to be sure the vaccine's effectiveness could be measured, and that others could manufacture it consistently and successfully. They knew that a Chicago pediatrician, Dr. Louis Sauer, also was preparing a pertussis vaccine in his office for his patients. But his methods and ingredients differed from theirs. Dr. Sauer used human blood in his vaccine. Grace and Pearl used blood from sheep kept in an old barn behind the Sunshine Hospital. They used heat to kill the pertussis bacteria included in their vaccine, while Dr. Sauer killed the bacteria with a substance called phenol. The two teams also used different numbers of bacteria per dose. The Michigan team realized they needed a sterile room—a room they could be sure was free of germs. They were able to move a little glassed-in cubicle from the laboratory in Lansing and install it in the middle of their lab. In developing a vaccine, conditions needed to be just right.

In the first report on Dr. Sauer's project, results looked good. Of the several hundred children who received his vaccine between 1928 and 1933, none contracted whooping cough. But Dr. Sauer had no control group. To really know how effective a treatment is, scientists need to compare the group of people getting a treatment to another, similar group that is not getting the treatment, known as a control group.

Work on the vaccine was intense. Grace said, "We went home for a hurried dinner and rushed back to the laboratory." They tested the sterility and safety of the vaccine. Pearl and Grace even gave themselves injections of some portions to be sure they were safe. "It's not a very scientific way of testing it," Grace said, "but we slept better afterwards."

But soon, they had to face a scarcity of money. They were short not only of funds but of staff. Early in the process, the Grand

Rapids City Commission allocated money to pay a bacteriologist. In 1935, money from private citizens, a federal relief agency, and the city commission funded salaries for a laboratory technician, a glassware worker, two nurses, two clerks, and an animal caretaker. Even so, the money was gone by September. Two dedicated workers stayed without pay until November, when a check from the Federal Works Progress Administration arrived. Around this time, the lab was graced by a visit from the president's wife, Eleanor Roosevelt. When photographers asked Mrs. Roosevelt to pose looking through a microscope, she refused politely and reached for a nearby baby to hold. A bold, active woman herself, who accomplished much during her husband's presidency, she apparently wanted her public image to seem more traditional.

The vaccine was almost ready. Now the researchers needed a control group. Pearl and Grace chose four thousand children in Kent County, Michigan, who were eight months to five years old. They split the children into two groups, making sure the groups contained children of similar age, social and economic background, and health. One group of two thousand was inoculated with the vaccine. The other two thousand—the control group—was not vaccinated. After forty-four months, they checked each child's health record. There were 348 cases of whooping cough in the control group and 52 cases in the vaccinated group. Doctors reported that in the vaccinated group, children who did come down with the disease had milder cases.

In October 1939, the Michigan Department of Health began to manufacture Grace and Pearl's vaccine. Subsequent tests confirmed that it was safe and effective. Today, after further improvements, it is over 90 percent effective.

The vaccine was the result of the efforts and contributions of many people. Pearl's staff volunteered extra time. Doctors cooperated by identifying patients and keeping inoculation records. Families risked their children's safety on a new and unknown vaccine. Local, state, and federal agencies helped finance the research during pitiful economic times. Kent County had gathered four thousand children to help test the vaccine. And behind it all were Grace and Pearl, who had dedicated themselves to the project, envisioned and guided it, worked a double shift at no extra pay, and even injected themselves to test their creation. However, unlike many vaccine inventors, Pearl and Grace declined the opportunity to have the vaccine named after them. They recognized that many people had been involved and that they could not have done it alone. It didn't feel right to claim all the credit.

The Kendrick/Eldering team went on to perfect a combination diptheria/pertussis/tetanus, or DPT, vaccine that is still given to infants all over the world. Pearl told a reporter, "It seemed possible to combine [the vaccines] to save the poor children all that discomfort."

Beyond her work on the vaccine, Pearl went on to assist other countries, the World Health Organization, UNICEF, and the Pan American Health Organization, traveling to Great Britain, Yugoslavia, Colombia, Chile, Brazil, Mexico, Uruguay, Venezuela,

Children in Costa Rica lining up to be vaccinated, 1952
—Courtesy Pan American Health Organization/World Health Organization

Panama, and Guatemala, among other places. She helped set up vaccination and immunization programs, advised national laboratories, and attended meetings and conferences. When Pearl left in 1951 to teach public health at the University of Michigan, Grace became associate director of Michigan's laboratories.

In 1960, the Michigan state legislature formally recognized Pearl's contributions to the health of the state. Pearl and Grace have also been honored by the Michigan Women's Hall of Fame and the world's scientific community.

Through their work, Pearl and Grace had become best friends. They bought a comfortable home together in Grand Rapids, with books and scientific journals stacked everywhere, cats, and a poodle. Outside there were wild birds to feed and flower gardens to tend. Grace and Pearl loved nature, especially Michigan's north country, and had found a summer cabin on Drummond Island, Michigan. By 1969, both women officially retired. They continued to write and publish scientific papers, participate in scientific associations, and keep up with copious reading. In their retirement, former coworkers remained some of their closest friends.

In 1980, Pearl died of bone cancer. She was ninety years old. Grace lived eight more years and died at age eighty-eight in their Grand Rapids home.

Both Pearl Kendrick and Grace Eldering recognized what interested them most in life and pursued it with passion. They held themselves to high standards and were lucky to find each other, sisters in science, along the way. We can still feel their impact on our lives today. As a reporter for the *Detroit Free Press* wrote, "If Grace had never met Pearl, you might not be alive."

Genevieve Gillette, during college
—Courtesy Michigan Department of Natural Resources

Genevieve Gillette

CHAMPION OF MICHIGAN PARKS

WHILE GENEVIEVE GILLETTE WAS A STUDENT at Michigan Agricultural College, World War I was raging in Europe. Many of her male classmates were away fighting. Some had been killed. Distraught and feeling powerless, Genevieve decided she needed to take action. She formed a student committee and chose a site west of Williams Hall, where students planted a tree in honor of each fallen classmate.

The effort was typical of Genevieve. She had a need to take action as well as an awareness of the comfort nature's beauty can bring. Throughout her life, she would work hard to protect that beauty and make it available to the people of Michigan. With her trademark hats and her picnic basket, Genevieve Gillette would become a symbol of nature conservation and preservation.

Born in 1898, Genevieve learned her love of nature from her family. Her father, David Gillette, grew up on a farm. For a while he worked as a sales manager, but the yearning to return to the soil grew too strong, and he quit his job. He moved his wife, Kitty, and their three-year-old, Genevieve, to a farm near Dimondale, Michigan, southwest of Lansing. There, in the spring, he took Genevieve in the horse-drawn wagon to see tiny pink and white arbutus flowers blooming, or he knelt by the brook and asked his daughter, "Can you hear what it says? It's talking to us." Glorious maple and beech trees on their Grand River property cast cool shade for picnics.

Genevieve's maternal grandmother, Mary Beal, lived nearby and often brought seeds and roots for them to plant. Brandishing a shovel taller than she was, Genevieve helped Mary dig and plant. They put a dark purple lilac near the new outhouse to sweeten the air. It grew to be spectacular, with heavy blossoms that gave off fragrant perfume. Its cuttings fostered many new bushes through the years. From Kitty, her mother, Genevieve learned the importance of sharing the beauty around them.

The year before Genevieve graduated from high school, her father died. It was one of the greatest sadnesses of Genevieve's life. Kitty sold the farm, and mother and daughter moved to a house on Sycamore Street in Lansing. Genevieve graduated from high school there in 1916. To support them, Kitty signed up for courses in law and business and then began charging fees for helping people with their finances. She also took in boarders to help pay for Genevieve's college expenses.

Genevieve enrolled at Michigan Agricultural College, now Michigan State University. She rode the streetcar to campus. One day, already sure of what interested her and what did not, Genevieve marched into their house and told her mother, "I'm not going to take what the girls are taking." She had mistakenly signed up for a class in home economics, and she was thoroughly repelled by it.

Fortunately, there were professors who supported her academic choices. Soon she was in a chemistry class, followed by other classes she enjoyed, including plant pathology—the study of plant diseases. An exhilarating new world opened to her. She learned about a course of study newly offered at the college, landscape architecture, and quickly enrolled in the classes. To her delight, she found she had a talent for drawing and painting—a necessity in this profession. Even while in school, she was able to put her new skills to use on campus. In addition to creating the memorial grove near Williams

Hall, Genevieve seeded a lawn and planted shrubs near what is today the Women's Intramural Building.

In 1920 Genevieve Gillette graduated, the first woman to earn a landscape architecture degree from an American college. That was also the year women won the right to vote. They chose shorter dresses, bobbed their hair, began dancing to fast music, and also started making inroads into the male professional world. Despite Genevieve's degree and the changing times, however, no Michigan landscape design firms hired her when she applied for jobs.

Instead, Genevieve accepted her only offer—from the famous Chicago architect of both buildings and landscapes, Jens Jensen. Then sixty years old, Jensen had moved to the United States from Denmark at age twenty-four. He was six feet tall with spiky white hair and a commanding personality. Working within the city park system, he had redesigned several major parks and established the biggest network of forest preserve and nature parks in any American city. He believed in "open spaces and sunshine" with lots of "living green." To Jensen, that meant planting only trees and plants native to the area. No palm trees in his midwestern designs! And native plants, which knew how to survive in their natural habitat, would thrive with less labor-intensive care, such as watering. Jensen also believed that everyone should have free access to parks.

Genevieve worked as Jenson's assistant, and he became her mentor and lifelong friend. She absorbed his ideas about designing recreational areas and preserving natural areas for education, recreation, and scientific purposes. She learned the meaning of the term "state park" from him. In the early 1920s, state parks were a relatively new concept. At that time Interlochen, in Grand Traverse County, was Michigan's only state park, and it was greatly appreciated and overused. Before this time, parks had been thought of simply as game refuges for hunters. Only later did people start thinking of parks as places for public recreation and enjoyment.

After Genevieve had worked in Chicago for four years, Jensen encouraged her to go home and promote a Michigan state park system.

In fact, she said, "He pestered me." Fortunately, when she got back to Michigan in 1924, she already had a friend in state government who was involved with parks. Whenever she had ridden the train home to visit her mother, she had also visited Peter J. Hoffmaster, one of her college classmates. P. J., as he was known, had returned from World War I to work for the very new State Parks Division in Michigan's Department of Conservation. With energy that bubbled over and ran down the side of the pot, Genevieve and P. J. schemed about how to obtain new land for parks. Like Genevieve and Jens Jensen, P. J. believed in public parks. In his first annual report as superintendent of Michigan's parks, P. J. wrote, "Park sites . . . are the pleasure grounds of everyone."

When Genevieve moved back to Michigan from Chicago, she found a job with Breitmeyer Flower Company and Nurseries in Detroit. The company had no landscape service and needed someone to answer the customer's many questions. Genevieve was the perfect person to dispense advice. Meanwhile, she worked on her dream of Michigan parks as a volunteer. In particular she believed that laborers, especially factory workers, needed and deserved the recreational opportunities parks had to offer.

Before leaving Chicago, Genevieve had also promised Jensen that she would start a Michigan chapter of Friends of Our Native Landscape, a group dedicated to preserving natural areas throughout the Midwest. She kept her promise, and the Friends began to meet. Soon, someone donated 350 acres of wild land near Ludington and Lake Michigan. After a few years, the Friends had raised enough money to establish a state park near Muskegon, eventually named after P. J. Hoffmaster. The park offered nearly three miles of Lake Michigan shoreline for beach lovers to explore.

Genevieve was so devoted to her conservation efforts that she could never see herself tending to a baby or domestic chores. She had become a tall, sturdy, energetic woman with stylish eyeglasses and a voice capable of booming. She was known for her honesty—saying what she meant and meaning what she said.

Genevieve and P. J. were close working partners. P. J. would tell Genevieve about a parcel of land that might make a good park. Genevieve would scout the parcels in her free hours. She would, she remembered, "go out loaded with detail maps. Sometimes I would get hold of two or three landscape students from Ann Arbor or East Lansing and we'd take off for a week or a weekend. We learned just what to look for and how to appraise it." They traveled cheaply, camping and cooking out. Genevieve sometimes went by herself or took her mother along. Later, in 1950, she would put together the Natural Areas Council to help with the scouting. The council is still active with Michigan parks today.

Genevieve resigned at Breitmeyer to consult for a year as a landscape architect in Lakeland, Florida. The chamber of commerce in Lakeland asked her "to please buy five hundred pounds of petunia seeds." But Genevieve's job was about more than petunias, and she let her employers know it. She replied, "I don't want any petunia nonsense. What we're going to use is city planning, not petunia seeds."

When she returned to Michigan the following year, she found work as a designer and landscaper for Detroit Parks and Recreation. Some of her assignments were a little unusual. Once, for a flower show, Genevieve designed an exhibit about the state's parks. In the large exhibition hall, she had boy scouts set up camp under real transplanted trees, and even had them cook and sleep there. For another show, Genevieve created a state tree nursery from which visitors could take home free pine seedlings.

In the late 1920s, Genevieve got involved with the Detroit Thrift Garden Project. A wealthy senator donated twelve thousand dollars to create vegetable gardens in the city. Millionaire automobile maker Henry Ford—whose wife, Clara, would become a close friend of Genevieve's—sent workers with tractors to plow up vacant lots. Genevieve was in her element, teaching people how to grow healthy plants. The gardens would save many people from going hungry or needing public assistance, especially when economic hard times hit with the Great Depression, starting in 1929.

Genevieve Gillette with President Lyndon Johnson
—Courtesy Michigan Department of Natural Resources

With much of the nation out of work, Genevieve was lucky in 1932 to find a job planning and landscaping a federal housing project called Westacres, in what is now West Bloomfield Township near Detroit. At Westacres, the government loaned families money to buy a house if they agreed to raise their own food. Each family received an acre of land to plant with vegetables and fruit trees. They could even raise chickens. Genevieve taught residents how to grow and preserve food. She oversaw the project, with its 150 houses and families, for eight years.

More and more, people recognized Genevieve as someone with opinions worth listening to. In 1935, when she was thirty-seven, a Detroit newspaper quoted her critique of the state's lack of funding for parks and conservation. Genevieve said, "Imagine playing host to nine million tourists every summer and having to beg [the legislature] year after year for funds." In another article, she was called "a saving angel to Michigan's natural beauty." Genevieve was a mover and shaker in Michigan society.

After her job with Westacres ended, Genevieve moved to Ann Arbor, home of the University of Michigan, and set up a private practice. For the next forty-five years, she designed landscapes for private homes, churches, universities, housing projects, parks, and industries. On the side, she continued her hard work on behalf of Michigan parks through these years. In 1951, she was saddened by the loss of her good friend and parks partner, P. J. Hoffmaster. Her mother, who had come to live with her in Ann Arbor in the late 1940s, died in 1955.

In the 1960s, Genevieve geared up for a new kind of work for the parks: lobbying the legislature. She realized that state legislators had to be convinced that citizens deserve clean, safe, recreation areas and that the state should provide these. Some parks were in a sad state of disrepair. Children were wading in sewer waste due to inadequate toilet facilities. Something had to be done. It wasn't easy; the legislature could be a mighty unfriendly place.

Genevieve became an expert lobbyist. Lawmakers respected and liked her, even if she intimidated a few. She was able to listen to other people and form relationships with them. She had the ability to motivate others and push them amicably into action. Stored in her head and heart was tremendous knowledge of parks and rec-reation in general, and of each of Michigan's parks in particular. In addition, Genevieve had a unique style that made people remember her. She traveled with a picnic basket filled not just with food but also with paperwork and journals. She also wore interesting, one-of-a-kind hats. That way, when phoning a legislator she had just met, she could say, "I'm the lady with the hat." Once she pulled feathers out of her hat for a legislator who liked to fly-fish, so he could use them as fish lures.

Genevieve founded the Michigan Parks Association (MPA) to focus on park rejuvenation. Skillfully, she drew other organizations into the effort, such as labor unions, women's clubs, and forestry associations. In 1968, the MPA won a huge victory. The Michigan legislature allocated one hundred million dollars of state money for the parks. No more begging for funds—at least for a while! But two of Genevieve's biggest battles still loomed ahead.

One of the state's most unspoiled areas lay on the far northwest tip of the Upper Peninsula: the wild Porcupine Mountains. P. J. Hoffmaster had first masterminded the establishment of a state park there. But lumber and mining companies, with their eyes on huge old trees and deposits of copper beneath the ground, wanted access to the park's riches. Challenging the companies and the legislators who supported them, Genevieve and the MPA worked hard for years. When they finally succeeded, the whole nation cheered.

Genevieve and the MPA also got involved in the National Park Service's effort to establish a national shoreline at Sleeping Bear Dunes, a beautiful state park along Lake Michigan near Empire. Sleeping Bear Dunes is a gorgeous area beside the intense blue waters of Lake Michigan, with 460-feet-tall sand dunes, trout streams, forests, and more. Genevieve said she would help the park service as long as they doubled the number of acres for the national shoreline. In her sixties at the time, Genevieve donned one of her hats, grabbed rolled-up surveys of the area, and headed for the capitols in Lansing and Washington, D.C. She crashed meetings and stalked the legislative halls.

Making Sleeping Bear Dunes into a national shoreline would affect people who already owned land there. Some families had been there for generations and were angry at the possibility of a federal takeover. But a large percentage of Michiganians wanted the land protected forever in the form of an expanded national park. The conflict raged for ten years. Finally, in late 1970, a compromise emerged that landowners could accept. Sleeping Bear Dunes National Shoreline was born.

During her later years, Genevieve was asked by President Lyndon Johnson to serve on the Citizen's Advisory Committee on Natural Beauty. She moved to Washington, D.C., and for four years in the late 1960s, threw herself into the work, chairing a national conference on scenic roads. Her success in this work won her awards.

Finally, tired and yearning for home, Genevieve resigned and moved back to Ann Arbor.

Genevieve's dynamic energy could no longer resist old age and infirmity. But if she could no longer lobby in person on behalf of parks and the environment, Genevieve still made dozens of phone calls and wrote letters. Fortunately, her good friend Christopher Graham looked after her. As a landscape architecture student, he had roomed at her house in 1975 and taken over many of her household duties. His help eased her old age, and she spent many peaceful hours in a favorite chair with a glass of iced tea, listening to the wrens sing. She died in May 1986.

During Genevieve's lifetime, the number of Michigan state parks grew from one to ninety-six. A few of her legacies are Tahquamenon State Park in the Upper Peninsula, with its cascades and tamaracks; Albert E. Sleeper State Park on Saginaw Bay; and wild Thompson State Park, purchased in part with Genevieve's life savings of $260,000. And, fittingly located in P. J. Hoffmaster State Park, the Genevieve Gillette Nature Center on Lake Michigan presents marvelous exhibits on nature and is open to all.

If you seek her monument, look about you.

Sippie Wallace during her recording career
—Courtesy Red Hot Jazz Archive

Sippie Wallace

THE DETROIT NIGHTINGALE

BEULAH BELLE THOMAS CAME INTO THE WORLD IN 1898, as the nineteenth century turned into the twentieth, in Houston, Texas. The eleventh of the thirteen Thomas children, she got her nickname, Sippie, when her front teeth were coming in—her family named her after the sipping noises she made when she ate.

As Sippie grew, a new style of American music also came into being: the blues. The blues mixed aspects of traditional African music with other types of music from early American black experience—the songs black slaves sang as they worked together; the spirituals with which they worshipped, that expressed their suffering and their hope; and even the songs with which black peddlers advertised their wares. The blues had a particular musical structure. Often, it sounded like call and response, with one person singing one phrase, and other voices answering. Blues lyrics were usually about sorrow, disappointment, bad luck, and misery. Eventually, the blues would be a major part of Sippie's life—but not quite yet.

Houston, a growing frontier town, had a large population of black laborers and domestics, including Sippie's parents, George and Fanny. Lively marching tunes and the syncopated rhythms of ragtime pulsed through the community. On Sundays, the air filled with church music. Music was something Sippie's family understood well. Her brother George Jr., thirteen years older, played the piano and organ and wrote music. He taught Sippie all of those skills. Her older sister Lillie coached her in singing. At a very young age, Sippie began singing solos at Shiloh Baptist Church, where her father, now passed away, had been a deacon. Hersal Thomas, a masterful pianist, was composing songs by the age of thirteen. There is some question as to whether Hersal was Sippie's baby brother or her nephew.

Soon the Thomas children began to hear that new, popular blues music. Their elders disapprovingly called it "wang-dang" music. Since the songs were often about love relationships, drinking, gambling, and other "sinful" behaviors, Fanny forbade her children to play, sing, or listen to it. But George and Lillie were fascinated by the new music. At night, they slipped away to play and learn the blues.

One Halloween when Sippie was in elementary school, she attended a vaudeville tent show that had set up around the corner near their house. Vaudeville, a type of variety theatre with musical, comic, and other acts, was the most popular form of entertainment at the time. Sippie even landed a small part in the show, as a young character called "Sister Give-a-Damn."

After that small taste of fame, Sippie was hooked. Though she was only about ten years old, she learned how to find out when tent shows would be in town and how to get herself noticed by them. Sometimes she played the piano. Finally, a dancer in one of the shows, Madame Dante, asked Sippie to be her personal maid and assist her during her snake charmer routine. It was Sippie's job to light the incense and, after Madame Dante's butterfly dance, to carry in Gary, a long snake coiled in a lidded basket. One time Gary stuck his head out of the basket early, while Sippie was carrying him. "I let that thing go and I flew," she remembered. The job paid a decent wage and Sippie was even able to travel around Texas with the show. Her mother and she reached an understanding since the income Sippie earned helped pay the family expenses.

In the early 1900s, adolescent Sippie began to sing with small bands. In 1914, when she was sixteen, Sippie's brother George left home for the New Orleans music scene. He quickly found a good job recording music for player pianos, and on the side he put together a band of his own as leader and piano player. He also started a successful music publishing business. After George married, Sippie joined his wife and him in New Orleans.

The Thomases lived in the Storyville section of New Orleans, a legendary quarter where sailors went to drink, eat, and carouse. The many establishments at which they did this employed musicians to keep the customers entertained. So Storyville also became a hotbed of musical innovation, a center of blues music as well as the birthplace of jazz.

Sippie relished the frequent jam sessions of ragtime and blues in her brother's living room, when musicians such as Louis Armstrong, King Oliver, Sidney Bechet, and Fats Waller dropped by with their instruments. She joined in, playing the piano sometimes and singing. Sippie turned out to be tiny, about five feet tall, but she had a big voice and knew how to use it. Pretty, with a well-rounded figure, she laughed often, revealing a signature gap between her front teeth. Fellow musicians who admired Sippie included the famous bluesman Fats Waller, who wrote a song for her entitled "Mama Gone Goodbye."

While living with George, Sippie fell in love with a man named Frank Beals and got married. But the marriage was a fiasco; it didn't last long. The following year, 1915, the U.S. Navy closed down the Storyville district. Many musicians lost their jobs and were forced to move away for work. Many went north to Memphis, Chicago, and Detroit. George chose to take his family and successful music publishing business to Chicago. Seventeen-year-old Sippie and young Hersal joined them.

But in 1918, when World War I ended, Sippie's mother died. Sippie, now twenty, returned for a time to Houston to be with her siblings. When she came back to Chicago, Sippie and her musical relatives worked hard to get on the roster with the Theater Owners Booking Association, or TOBA. TOBA was an agency that found work for performers on the black vaudeville circuit. With TOBA, Sippie became a star. The railroad car on which she traveled between cities bore a banner advertising her as "The Texas Nightingale." She toured across the country, from New York to San Francisco. Sometimes she made fifty dollars a week—a tidy wage for the time. Meanwhile, when she was home in Chicago, she, George, and Hersal lived and breathed the blues. George's daughter Hociel was also shaping up into a fine singer, keeping the family's musical tradition alive.

One day, the general manager of OKeh Records, Ralph Peer, visited George and his family in Chicago. OKeh was a New York label with a branch known as OKeh Race Records, specializing in black performers for black audiences. Peer was looking for a blues singer to make records. George turned to Sippie, who was between bookings, and asked teasingly, "Do you think you could sing the blues?" Of course he knew she could.

Sippie's heart must have leaped for joy. She had devoted more than half her life in pursuit of just such a moment. She sang for Peer, George made a demonstration record, and Sippie signed a contract with OKeh. Between 1923 and 1929, Sippie Wallace reached stardom as a blues singer—performing the music her parents had considered sinful. Sippie's first phonograph record had on one side the wailing tune "Up the Country Blues," which she had written, and on the other side, a song called "Shorty George." The record sold a hundred thousand copies—the same as "going platinum" today. In all, with Sippie singing, accompanied by George and/or Hersal, the Thomases would record about two dozen records of their own songs and more by other songwriters.

An OKeh Race Records newspaper ad promoting another of Sippie's songs read, "Sippie Wallace delivers the 'Underworld Blues' . . . it is some powerful, wicked blues and no mistake. It's probably the most sobbin'est, weepin'est, moanin'est blues you ever heard.

Trot down to the nearest OKeh dealers and get it." In the photograph, Sippie looks glamorous in a huge hat of peacock feathers.

During these years, Sippie made a lot of money and led the life of an entertainment queen. It was rare at that time for recording artists to exercise much control over their work sessions, but Sippie remembered her producers coming to her and saying, "Who do you want to play [with you] today?" She almost always chose Hersal as a band member, and she didn't forget her old friends from Storyville—Joe Oliver, Louis Armstrong, and others. More than half her songs were instant hits.

"Sometimes Ralph Peer's secretary, Gertrude, would hand me a song with a hundred-dollar bill pinned to it and say, 'Sing this one,'" Sippie remembered. They believed that, sung by Sippie, the song would surely become a moneymaker. But Sippie enjoyed singing her own songs, too—songs such as "Mighty Tight Woman":

> If you're a married man
> You ain't got no business here
> 'Cause when you're out with me
> I might make your wife shed tears
> 'Cause I'm a mighty tight woman
> And there is nothing that I fear.

Requests for stage appearances flooded in. Sippie appeared in gorgeous gowns with plunging necklines, rich fabrics, sequins, and feathers. Her stage presence was mischievous and spirited, and audiences loved the expressiveness with which she sang.

Sippie took pleasure in entertaining and giving lavish dinners. Her friends included Sara Martin, another OKeh blues singer and former vaudevillian, and Victoria Spivey, a multitalented musician and performer and Houston native like Sippie. There was also a handsome black couple, Jodie Edwards and Susie Hawthorne, who performed comedy as the duo Butterbeans and Susie. On stage and on OKeh recordings with Louis Armstrong and others, they bickered hilariously. As a husband and wife in real life, they were easygoing and devoted to each other.

Sippie's career peaked in 1925. The next year, she married Matt Wallace, a dapper, charismatic gambler from Houston. Matt became Sippie's manager and even cowrote two songs with her. Sippie adored her new husband, but eventually his gambling would lead to financial trouble for her. Also in 1926, Sippie's beloved Hersal died of food poisoning, a terrible shock to her. Sippie's personal world had begun to crumble. The year before, her sister Lillie had also died, and not long after, George was struck by a Chicago streetcar and killed. Sippie's nearest, dearest relatives and teachers—gone forever! Her song "Bedroom Blues" tells of abandonment:

> Lord, I tried to cry but my tears refused to fall.
> Lord, I tried to cry but my tears refused to fall,
> I was all alone, no one to love me at all.

The religion of her youth helped Sippie make it through this difficult time.

Sippie kept recording, but in February of 1929, after she cut four songs for Victor Records and only two songs sold, she had to accept that her fortune had changed. The economic crash that led to the Great Depression effectively ended Sippie's stardom.

Before the crash, Sippie and Matt had moved to Detroit's east side. Matt worked as a day laborer when he could, while Sippie went back to touring and performing. For the first time, she booked her own appearances, finding that she could make more money than she had with TOBA. By 1932, however, all her theatrical contacts had dried up, and in 1937, her beloved Matt died of pneumonia. Sippie was thirty-nine years old.

Sippie gave up performing, at least at the level she once had. Unfortunately, much of the money she had once earned was gone. She had entrusted it to George and her husband, Matt. Neither of them proved worthy of her trust. George had cashed her checks, giving her only a portion back. Matt had gambled much of her money away. Her recording company had also exploited Sippie. For one thing, she was never paid separately for the songs she had written, as a songwriter should have been.

Years of modest, careful living lay ahead of Sippie. For the rest of her life, it seemed, the only creative outlet she would have was making music at her church, Leland Baptist, where she directed the choir, wrote music, played the piano, and sang. Nor would she ever remarry, though she did find another man to share her life with—Buddy Taylor, who lived with her until his death in 1974.

Fast-forward nearly thirty years, to 1965. The times have changed again. Mainstream America and even Europe have become wildly interested in folk music—including the blues. Many of the people who invented the blues are still alive, like Sippie, now sixty-seven years old.

One Saturday, Sippie's phone rang. A European promoter wanted to know if she could perform in London. Within forty-eight hours she was in Chicago, waiting for the flight. Night after night Sippie, now plump and grandmotherly, enchanted sold-out British audiences with classics like "Don't Advertise Your Man" and "Woman Be Wise."

Sippie Wallace in performance during the second blossoming of her career
—Michigan Women's Historical Center and Hall of Fame

The following year, she recorded an album with her old friend Victoria Spivey. Spivey, who had always had good business sense, saw no reason why the performers who had originated the blues shouldn't take advantage of the music's current popularity. She started a record company and recorded many of her old friends.

Around this time, a Wayne State University freshman entered Sippie's life. Ron Harwood loved the blues and was majoring in ethnomusicology (the study of the music of various cultures). One day he looked up Sippie's number in the phone book and scheduled a visit. For a month he interviewed her and listened to her perform. He decided to join forces with Sippie and help her make a comeback. He learned about contracts and became her manager. "My mother had to cosign the contract for me," he remembered, because he was so young. But he was determined to protect Sippie from the exploitation she had experienced before.

At Chicago's huge blues festival in 1967, the crowd gave Sippie a standing ovation before she even sang a note. That same year held a particularly poignant moment for Sippie. Before a concert at the University of Detroit, she met Louis Armstrong again for the first time in decades. Ron Harwood remembered that Louis was sitting by himself on the stage during a break in the rehearsal. When he looked up, he saw Sippie, and his eyes got big.

"Sippie Wallace!" he exclaimed.

They hugged for five minutes, then Louis turned to Ron and told him, "I used to play for this woman. She was a star, a big star, and don't you ever forget it!"

At last, Sippie was getting the international attention and appreciation she deserved. But when she was seventy-six, a massive stroke paralyzed her. She couldn't even speak, and lay in bed for three months. It was six months before she could begin to move around. As soon as she could, she went to the piano and played—all day. Wondrously, her ability to make music had returned.

After her stroke, Sippie went back to performing. She sang from a wheelchair the first time she shared a stage with young white singer Bonnie Raitt, with whom she immediately became fast friends. The bluesy Raitt said, "Sippie has an incredible musical sense . . . She was a truly liberated woman and her lyrics display a remarkable sensitivity." The two accomplished women performed together frequently.

On her eighty-fourth birthday, long free of her wheelchair, Detroit's living legend enjoyed a two-day celebration with Raitt, pianist Dr. John, and the Little Chicago Jazz Band in Ann Arbor. The next night, at a performance in Detroit's Grand Circus Theater, the audience sang "Happy Birthday" to Sippie. By now, Sippie had diabetes and her fingers trembled sometimes, but she belted out her songs with the heart of a young woman.

Four years later to the day, on her eighty-eighth birthday, Sippie Wallace passed on at last. She left a treasure trove of music that she sang and wrote from the depths of her being while shaping one of America's few original art forms: the blues.

Young Cora Brown —State Archives of Michigan

10 Cora Brown

FIRST BLACK WOMAN IN A STATE SENATE

CORA BROWN'S FRIENDS AND POLITICAL OPPONENTS agreed on one thing about her: Cora's smile brightened whatever corner she happened to be in. More importantly, she was an independent thinker. She came to her own conclusions and held firmly to her beliefs.

Cora Mae Brown was born in 1914 in Alabama. She was an only child, a rarity at a time when large families were common. Her parents, Richard and Alice, lavished attention on their lively daughter. Her father was a tailor, a better-paying occupation than most black men had in those days, just fifty years after the end of slavery. He and Alice valued Cora's opinions and wanted a better life for her than they had been able to have. Because of her parents, Cora grew up with considerable self-esteem.

When Cora was a small child, the Brown family lived in the small villages of Bessemer and Blossburg, Alabama. But recognizing that opportunities for jobs and education would be better in a city, the family moved to Birmingham, where Cora entered kindergarten.

The family's hopes for a better life did not materialize, however. By the time Cora was seven, times had become hard for the Browns. Cora's grandparents, who lived up north, urged in their letters, "Come to Michigan. People here have money to support a tailor." Richard and Alice pulled out their suitcases and packed up their belongings.

The Browns migrted to Detroit and rented a house in a racially mixed neighborhood at 961 Alfred Street. On the first day of school, Alice walked Cora to Bishop School and enrolled her. Meanwhile, Richard set up a tailor shop and began building a profitable business. In 1922, Detroit's auto industry offered jobs to all races of workers, unlike some places and industries. The money these jobs put in workers' pockets helped pay for the other services they needed—such as those of a tailor.

When Cora was about eleven, she had her first experience with bigotry. At school, a white boy a bit older than her called Cora a "schwarze," which means "black woman" in German. From his sneering intonation, she could tell he didn't mean it as a compliment. With all her might, Cora wheeled around and punched him in the face. There was no report of Cora punching another child again. Her schoolmates must have learned the proper way to speak to her.

In 1931, Cora graduated from Cass Technical High School. A friend of the family had graduated from Fisk University in Nashville, Tennessee, and recommended it to Cora. Fisk, one of the nation's most prestigious black universities, had been founded soon after the Civil War. Cora entered Fisk that fall.

With her usual determination, Cora decided she wanted to make a career of medicine. One of the first courses she had to take was health education. One day when she entered the classroom for the lecture, a dead body lay on a table. Cora turned green and ran out of the classroom. When she learned that a medical education includes learning internal anatomy from cadavers, Cora quickly changed her major to sociology.

Cora left Fisk with her diploma in hand in 1935. It was the middle of the Great Depression, the dreadful economic crash that started in 1929. Jobs were few, and hardship was abundant. But Cora's career choice was lucky, as it turned out. The government needed social workers to assist the thousands of unemployed people in Detroit. Cora joined the ranks of Detroit's social workers. She would stay in this career for five years.

In 1940, Cora put her background in sociology to work in a new occupation: as a policewoman with the Women's Division of the Detroit Police. Much of her work consisted of preparing paperwork for legal cases. In 1943, however, something happened that made a huge impression on her and would determine new directions in her professional life.

At that time, Detroit already had a history of racial conflict. Although factories were glad to hire black workers, blacks faced poor circumstances in most other aspects of their lives. Like many other American cities, Detroit was tightly segregated. In the part of town where most black people lived—called, ironically, Paradise Valley—living conditions were terrible.

One hot summer night in 1943, fights broke out between whites and blacks in Detroit's elegant recreational park, Belle Isle. From there, the violence spread. The next day, thousands of federal troops occupied the city. They would stay for six months. Nine whites and twenty-five blacks died during the riots. Seventeen of the twenty-five blacks who died were killed by white policemen. Nationwide, the riots were blamed largely on the blacks.

Cora interviewed a woman who was being held in jail for investigation after the riots. The woman's children were home alone. Under such circumstances, it was normal police department policy to arrange for the children's care. But when Cora telephoned the Ninth Precinct police station to send someone for the children, the officer in charge said, "I don't give a damn what happens to these Negroes who started this race riot."

Cora was incensed. A prejudiced adult with power was willing to let innocent children suffer. Cora worked out the childcare problem on her own, but she never forgot the incident.

Cora thought about other cases she had encountered at work in which clients in need received little or no aid. She also thought about her dealings as a policewoman with Recorder's Court, where criminal cases were tried. Every encounter she had had with the court fascinated her. She decided there and then: she would become an attorney. In criminal law, there are two types of attorneys: defense lawyers, who represent people accused of crimes, and prosecutors, whose job it is to convict accused people and send them to jail. Cora had seen too many accused people treated unfairly by those in power. She chose to become a defense attorney.

Cora entered Wayne State University's law school in 1946. Two years later, she graduated and passed the state bar exam. A lawyer now, Cora became partners with another woman in Detroit, Alice Jones Morris, and began practicing as a defense attorney. Her new career satisfied her desire to defend underprivileged people. She felt proud to have their trust, her knowledge of the law, and a meaningful job. She also had her own home. Her father had died in 1943, and her mother, Alice, now lived with her.

However, Cora was a person driven to make a difference, and it wasn't long before the political arena beckoned. She helped found a Democratic delegates' council in one of Detroit's state congressional districts. The council promoted the beliefs and goals of the Democratic political party in the district—beliefs and goals to which Cora felt strongly committed. Serving as the council's secretary for a term, Cora began learning the ins and outs of politics. In 1950, an election year for the state senate, a seat opened up in Michigan's Second District. Desiring to contribute as much as possible to her home state, Cora geared up to run.

During the campaign, in an interview with a journalist, Cora spoke politely yet honestly about the present congressmen's attitude toward women colleagues. "Women politicians are not exactly wanted [because] it is generally felt that, peculiar to their sex, they may not understand the workings [of government] and will refuse to go along with them."

Cora's opponent was another Democrat, Anthony J. Wilkowski. Wilkowski was an incumbent. He already held the office and was running for re-election. Sadly, Cora lost the race. Seven thousand votes went to Wilkowski versus Cora's humble seven hundred. But in the end, Wilkowski never served his term. The Michigan senators refused to readmit him to the Senate because of his past election fraud. Another election for his seat would have to be held.

When the special election to replace Wilkowski took place in 1951, Cora tried again. This time she lost to Bristoe Bryant, a popular disc jockey with access to a wide radio audience.

Cora went back to making a fine living as a lawyer. Now thirty-seven years old, she had not married. She lived comfortably with her mother on Chestnut Street in Detroit and enjoyed cooking and homemaking. However, politics had a magnetism she could not resist.

The primary election for state senators came up in 1953. Voters from each party would choose their candidate for the final (general) election. Cora tried again. Greatly wiser after the trouncings she had suffered in the past, she hired a sound truck to roll through neighborhoods and broadcast her name and what she stood for. She went door to door and spoke with hundreds of people, campaigning for better hospital facilities and social services in Wayne County, issues her work had made her intimately familiar with. She was also concerned about the inequalities black Americans faced. The Civil Rights movement had not yet started—it was just around the corner. Ahead of her time, Cora pushed for the betterment of black people's lives and future.

Cora won the election! Exhilarated, "the handsome politician and lawyer," as one reporter described her, took her oath of office for Michigan's Second Senatorial District and began her term on January 14, 1953. In an interview on the day of her victory, Cora urged women to take an active interest in politics. "Women have always been able to bring sound and humane reasoning into everyday life. I believe they are the hope of the century. And yes, I have my ideas to better certain aspects of state government, but I'll learn the ropes first."

Learning the ropes didn't take Cora long. Soon a *Lansing State Journal* article recounted one of her first accomplishments in office. The article described how soft-spoken Cora, the "first woman of her race to sit on the Senate and the second woman in history to be elected to that body, won a hands down victory in the chamber Thursday after less than two months of legislative experience."

Cora had opposed a bill that would have forced defense attorneys to disclose the names, addresses, and occupations of character witnesses for trials. The bill had been introduced by Republican senator Don Gilbert, who had been a prosecutor. Gilbert had a reputation for quick, sharp comments and for grandstanding and showing off during debates. Cora debated Gilbert, arguing that the bill violated citizens' civil rights. It would allow police departments and prosecutors to abuse witnesses, scaring them away before a trial. The bill failed, and Cora triumphed. Clearly, she did not intend to merely dabble her feet in congressional waters. She dove in headfirst.

Cora went on to propose a bill to increase penalties for hotels, restaurants, and motels that discriminated against people of color. A law forbidding racial discrimination already existed, but many felt it was too lax. Her bill upped the fine for violations from twenty-five to one hundred dollars. Also, the existing law did not apply to motels. Cora saw to it that the new bill did. Her bill passed with a huge majority.

Cora must have felt elated with her success. The tenderfoot female legislator had confronted an established, powerful colleague, Don Gilbert, and prevailed. Her civil rights legislation had won. In her new job as senator, she found she had a natural ability to deal easily and effectively with her colleagues.

Cora worked on senate committees concerned with public utilities, health, and welfare. She made frequent appearances on television and radio, letting the public know how she stood on popular issues. She was not afraid to disagree with anyone, including other Democrats or people of her own race. If she disagreed, she said so plainly and explained why. When the next election came along in 1954, Cora made a strong showing and won another two-year term.

For the next election in 1956, however, Cora decided to switch districts. She wanted to run in the first district, not the second, where she had won her past two elections. This surprised her colleagues. The first-district seat was held by another Democrat, Thaddeus Machrowicz. Machrowicz had served in two wars and worked as an attorney and municipal judge. He enjoyed considerable acclaim among his constituents.

For the election, Cora used her usual campaign methods, which had brought her success in the past. This time, however, the United Auto Workers (UAW), a powerful labor union, did not back her. Nor did the Democratic Party. During the preceding year, following her conscience, Cora had asked black citizens not to vote for Democratic congressmen who would not publicly oppose congressional chairmen who were against civil rights. This probably cost Cora her party's and the UAW's support. Cora lost the election by a large margin.

What Cora Brown thought still carried weight, however, even though she was no longer a senator. Therefore, her Democratic colleagues were astounded when she came out in support of Republican president Dwight Eisenhower for re-election. In 1952, Cora had supported Democratic presidential candidate Adlai Stevenson instead of Eisenhower. But later, when Stevenson went south to speak and campaign with Southern Democrats, he lost Cora's support. "It was obvious to me," she said, "that he'd become acceptable to the people who wanted segregation."

As a way of sealing her commitment to President Eisenhower, Cora went to Washington, D.C., to talk with him. She felt he was sympathetic toward civil rights, but she wanted to be sure. Her friend Jessie Vann, a seasoned journalist and owner of the black newspaper, the *Pittsburgh Courier*, accompanied her. The two women visited with the president for thirty-five minutes. Cora left the White House with her commitment in place, though she told reporters she was still a Democrat and, in Michigan, would support the Democratic candidate for governor.

Cora Brown, legislator
—Michigan Women's Historical
Center and Hall of Fame

Eisenhower did support some advances for black people. During his presidency, more black faces appeared in high- and mid-level positions than under any previous administrations. In 1957, one of those faces belonged to Cora Brown. U.S. Postmaster General Arthur Ellsworth Summerfield appointed Cora to the legal staff of the federal Post Office Department. For about four years, Cora worked as associate general counsel. She specialized in problems connected to pornography distribution and the use of mail to defraud.

Cora's mother had remarried several years before and was well situated, so, after her stint with the Post Office Department, Cora decided to move to Los Angeles, California. There she opened a law office and practiced for ten years. But in 1971, at age fifty-seven, Cora came home to Detroit. Politics was no longer her hobby, as she put it, so running for office didn't cross her mind. Instead, she accepted an appointment to the Michigan State Unemployment Commission. There, she worked as a referee, or mediator. When workers became unemployed and there were differences with the employer, Cora listened to and worked with both sides. But she wasn't able to enjoy the job for long. She died of cancer and meningitis at Grace Hospital in December 1972 and was buried at Elmwood Cemetery in Detroit.

In following her own high ethics, Cora Mae Brown was a thorn in the conscience of Michigan politicians and even a president. Before the Civil Rights and Women's movements, she broke through the strong double barrier of race and gender. Her dedication to civil rights for all helped build a road for women and people of color to travel into the land of politics—and anywhere else they might choose.

Myra Wolfgang (left) at work —Walter P. Reuther Library

Myra Wolfgang

FOR THE LOVE OF LABOR

WIND PUTS ELEMENTS IN MOTION, even if it sometimes causes storms. In the world of labor unions in Detroit from the 1930s until her death in 1975, Myra Wolfgang was a whirlwind of action and change. Ardent throughout her life about adequate wages, benefits, and quality of work life for workers, Myra started at the bottom as a union employee and worked her way to the top. Along the way, the *Detroit News* called her "the most effective leader for the working poor in Michigan."

Myra was born Mira Komaroff in 1914 in Montreal, Canada. Her parents were both Jewish immigrants—her father, Abraham, from Russia, and her mother, Ida, from Lithuania. Before Mira was born, Ida and Abraham believed in the importance of workers in the world's economy and in life. The Komaroffs were married not in a synagogue, but in Montreal's Labor Temple, the hall where workers met. "Labor" refers generally to workers, and especially, to the organizations that represent them.

The Komaroffs had three children, Michael, Sarah, and Mira. When Mira was a year old, the family moved to Detroit, where Abraham sold real estate for a living. After World War I ended in 1918, prosperity returned to the United States, and Mira's family moved into a large, beautiful home on Westminster Avenue. The house was filled with fine rugs, handsome, comfortable furniture, shelves of books, and a grand piano. With their children and visiting guests, Abraham and Ida discussed the social issues of the day, including labor reform. Ida also believed in the equality of women. She told her daughters, "Any woman with a mind should use it." Ida took the children to museums, libraries, concerts, and ballets.

When the economic crash of the Great Depression hit the United States, Mira was a student at Detroit's Northern High School. Abraham's business declined, and the family moved into a small rental house. Mira's brother and sister had already been through college, but Mira would have to fend for herself. Luckily, she had been raised to be independent. After graduating from high school in 1931, Mira enrolled at Carnegie Institute in Pittsburgh to study commercial art and interior design. She worked as a waitress to pay her expenses. By the end of the year, though, her job waiting tables fell through and she couldn't find another. She dropped out of school and moved back to Detroit.

Now eighteen, Mira was tall and attractive. She parted her dark hair in the middle and pulled it back in a classic style. Her broad face had high cheekbones, a pert nose, and lively brown eyes, and when she smiled, it was like the sun coming out from behind a cloud. Her dark good looks attracted attention, and back in Detroit she made quite an impression as she stood in the middle of crowds making speeches on behalf of a political candidate, Al Renner. Renner, a clerk and accountant, was running for governor of Michigan with the Proletarian Party. The Proletarian Party was critical of the American political system. Focused on giving the working class—particularly industrial workers—more power, the party's beliefs were rooted in communist and socialist theory and the ideas of German philosopher Karl Marx. For example, Socialists believed private, individual ownership of business and industry should be replaced by larger, societal control. These ideals attracted Mira.

One early summer day, attending an automobile workers' meeting at Cass Technical High School, Mira met Louis

Koenig, secretary-treasurer of the Detroit Waiters Union Local 705. (A "local" is a branch of the larger union. The Waiters Union still exists today as the Hotel Employees and Restaurant Employees Union.) The next morning, when Local 705's bustling office opened, an uninvited, determined Mira stepped in and volunteered to help. Before the workday ended, Koenig had hired her as a receptionist-secretary-bookkeeper for fifteen dollars a week. Euphoric, Mira threw herself into her new job.

In 1932, Franklin Delano Roosevelt unseated Herbert Hoover during the presidential election. Roosevelt was progressive, so labor activists were ecstatic. It was time for better labor laws in the United States. Louis Koenig and his new protégé, Mira Komaroff, would make sure Local 705 helped enact that change.

As she had done for Al Renner, Mira took to the streets on behalf of Local 705, promoting workers' participation in unions. Not yet old enough to vote in an election, she nonetheless spoke with feeling and authority and urged working people to unite. She spoke from truck beds and from the steps of City Hall, calling attention to industry leaders who took more than their share. Mira's fresh energy and the ease and vibrancy with which she spoke led some to call her "La Passionata." La Passionata was a famous female fighter in the civil war then raging in Spain who became famous for the quote, "It is better to die on your feet than live forever on your knees." Newspapers also dubbed Mira "the Battling Belle of Detroit."

Meanwhile, Mira efficiently ran the Local 705 office, making it possible for Koenig and other associates to recruit hotel and restaurant workers. The local was also focused on repeal of the Eighteenth Amendment. Passed in 1918, this national law prohibited the manufacture, sale, or transport of alcohol in the United States and had ushered in the era known as Prohibition. In response, saloons and taverns went into hiding. These illegal drinking establishments earned such nicknames as "blind pigs" and "speakeasies," and the police found it impossible to suppress them. In Detroit, "rum runners" sneaked alcohol across the river from Canada. Prohibition created a bad situation for wait staff and bartenders because they could be taken advantage of. Employers might pay them only pennies a day, but they couldn't complain since they themselves were breaking the law by working there. Repeal of the amendment would not only make these jobs legitimate again, it would create many more jobs, so badly needed during the Depression. The following year, 1933, the amendment was repealed.

Labor made more strides as Roosevelt attempted to help the nation's economy. Under the National Industrial Recovery Act, employees gained the right to organize themselves and bargain as a group with their employer. A new government agency forced businesses to pay a federal minimum wage and limited work hours. Detroit celebrated. Happy and hopeful, fifteen thousand people paraded down Woodward Avenue.

In their struggles with unscrupulous employers, unions had to come up with ingenious strategies to get their points across. Strikes and picketing were their main strategies. In a strike, laborers simply refused to work until their demands were met. Outside their workplaces, they paraded or stood with large signs stating their grievances. Workers lost wages during a strike, but—usually—embarrassment and loss of business brought employers quickly to the bargaining table. There were many risks associated with striking, though. Workers might be harassed, injured, or jailed. They might be absent from their families for long periods of time during a strike. And if the strike failed, workers could lose their jobs.

Mira led her first strike in front of the Fox Restaurant. The waitresses were picketing for better wages and working conditions and quickly won. How Mira relished her first success as a leader! But she took her lumps, too. At Charlie Shannon's Bar, she and other picketers were jailed and released twice in one day before the owner signed a contract. Local 705 rewarded Mira in 1934 with a promotion—though her wages remained at fifteen dollars a week.

Not yet twenty-one, Mira lived with her family in a small, crowded apartment. In 1935 she moved into her own apartment on Selden Street, a single room with a bed that pulled down from the wall.

Mira began to tire of the heavy duties of managing an office. She longed to get back to speaking and organizing on the streets, and she spoke to Koenig about representing Local 705. Part of her job would be to talk to restaurant and hotel owners. She argued that they might respond better to a courteous young woman than to a middle-aged man. Koenig gave her the go-ahead. When Mira met with managers and owners, she found they often patronized her until she pointed out how they overworked and underpaid their employees. She tried to get employers to see how they would actually benefit if their workers organized. They could be sure, for example, that a Local 705 worker was well qualified for a job. If all else failed, she reminded employers about picket lines, which chased away customers.

In 1936, Koenig hired a new organizer, a young waiter, to organize strikes and picket lines. The new employee earned thirty dollars a week, which was soon raised to forty-five dollars. Mira fumed. After almost four years on the job working ten- to twelve-hour days, she was getting the same fifteen-dollar-a-week wage she had started at. She deserved a salary equal—at least—to her new male coworker's. She argued with Koenig until he gave in.

Meanwhile, Local 705 was making headway. One strike at the St. Moritz Restaurant was particularly effective. Waiters, waitresses, bartenders, and cooks set up a picket line. Inside, one of Mira's Local 705 coworkers suggested that the bartender "fix the drinks." When some policemen broke through the picket line and went inside, they took advantage of the situation and quickly downed a few drinks—as the organizers knew they would. In a minute, they were dashing for the restroom. The drinks had been fixed with a substance that made them sick. On the spot, the horrified restaurant owner promised to hire all his workers through the union office.

The first major strike Mira organized was a sit-down at the Woolworth's store at Woodward and Grand River Avenues in

Detroit. Mira and other union organizers ushered startled customers outside the store, then locked the doors. Union members outside kept others from coming in. For the next seven days, striking sales-clerks and restaurant waitresses occupied the store. A speaker who Mira brought in to keep up the strikers' morale, Frances Comfort of Detroit's Federation of Teachers, reminded them,

> You find yourselves here behind a counter working for hopeless pay. You are fighting, not only for yourselves, but for thousands of girls like yourselves, all through the country.

The union brought in meals, and a *Life* magazine photographer came and snapped pictures, which appeared the following week in the magazine. As time wore on, the strikers couldn't keep from demolishing the store's stock of Easter candy. In the end, they won a raise, a forty-eight-hour week, and a week's vacation after a full year's employment.

During the 1930s, strikes erupted all over Detroit—so many that newspapers began publishing daily lists of closed businesses, offices, restaurants, and hotels. Meanwhile, Mira and her cohorts came up with new ways to persuade employers to provide better working conditions in restaurants and hotels. One strategy was called a "customer strike."

Choosing a restaurant where General Motors executives lunched and a waitress's wage was $1.17 a day, two hundred Local 705 members filed into the restaurant before lunchtime, took seats, and ordered coffee. When the hungry executives arrived and saw it was filled, they left. Incensed, the restaurant owner called the police, but when they arrived, they found only peaceful customers sitting over cups of cold coffee. They could do nothing about it. The owner agreed to union hiring policies and decent conditions for workers.

Mira's union was against racial discrimination. Its laws decreed that "any competent person working in the allied crafts was eligible for membership in the Alliance." In 1941, white unionists picketed alongside black waiters on strike against the Detroit Athletic Club. Because of Mira, Local 705 was integrated at a time when many unions were actively shutting out blacks and preserving jobs for white members. Mira was a life member of the National Association for the Advancement of Colored People, or NAACP.

One incident provided Mira with an extraordinary chance to showcase the professionalism of the union waiter—and at the same time, demonstrate her own ability to organize people. Ford Motor Company was giving a lunch for eight thousand dealers at the Detroit Coliseum, and that same evening, a dinner for five thousand. Myra arranged for and prepared 548 servers. The wait staff whipped meals to the tables at an incredible three per second!

In 1936, when Mira was twenty-two, Michigan governor Frank Murphy appointed her to the Domestic and Personal Department of the Michigan Employment Security Commission, or MESC. The position was an honor, and the hours, salary, and benefits were greatly superior to her union job. Still, Mira accepted the government post with the condition that she could continue, part-time, with Local 705. After a day of work at the MESC, Mira would dash for the Local 705 office, or take a bus to one of the soup kitchens the unions ran for workers on strike.

At twenty-four, Mira chose to give her personal life more attention. She had a sweetheart, attorney Moe Wolfgang. There was nothing not to like about this handsome Jewish man, whose quiet inward strengths equaled Mira's more outgoing ones in power. Thirty-year-old Moe accepted Mira's allegiance to her work. Mira and Moe married in 1939 in a small ceremony at Detroit's Book-Cadillac Hotel. Mira made one concession to the new change in her life: she resigned from her MESC job. With their two paychecks, the newlyweds moved into a nice apartment. Mira's father had died of a heart attack a few years earlier, and the couple was even able to help Mira's mother and unmarried sister financially.

Mira took a leave of absence from the union office in 1942 when her daughter Laura was born. Delighted, Moe became a loving caregiver. Around this time, Mira officially changed the spelling of her name to Myra. As a new mother, she scaled down her work and stopped drawing a salary from Local 705. But she continued to attend union board meetings, and Koenig phoned daily to discuss important negotiations. World War II was raging, and service workers did not have it easy. The War Board froze wages to as low as forty cents an hour, yet prices for food, fuel, and other goods kept rising due to wartime shortages.

After the birth of a second daughter, Martha, and with the help of Moe and a housekeeper, Myra eased back into union work. In 1948, she began what would be a sixteen-year fight for a state minimum wage. She never let up, writing letters and speeches and pestering legislators and governors. "Michigan is the only northern state that does not have a minimum wage law," she reminded them. Years later, she would remark, "I've been campaigning for [a minimum wage] for so long that when I pick up my briefcase and see the initials M. W., I don't know whether they stand for Myra Wolfgang or minimum wage."

The remark was typical of Myra's wit. For her work, Myra traveled and made specches throughout the country. People either loved her biting sense of humor and her gutsiness or they hated it. One time she reminded an audience of mostly male dignitaries, "Women were in labor long before you were born." As she aged, she never lost her attractiveness and wore flamboyant, colorful clothes.

To women in the Feminist movement, which began emerging in the 1960s, Myra became a figure of controversy. She agreed with feminist leader Betty Friedan and the National Organization for Women on such issues as equal pay for equal work and access to childcare and abortion. But she was against the Equal Rights Amendment, or ERA, which would have guaranteed men and women equal rights under the constitution. She called the ERA "a bid for equal mistreatment for women that men now suffer, such as unrestricted overtime work." Speaking to a women's club in the 1970s, Myra would later say,

[The Women's Liberation Movement] has failed to recognize that class makes a difference in women's goals. . . . Middle class women seek equality, while lower class women fight to end exploitation. . . . One goal that's shared by working class women is *not* to have to work. . . . It's only for middle class women that work is liberating.

In 1960, two exciting dreams came true. First, Myra became the top executive of Local 705 when Louis Koenig retired. Second, Myra coordinated the Detroit Waiters and Waitresses Training School. The next year, 150 graduates in dinner jackets or elegant black dresses and white aprons received their diplomas while Myra looked on proudly.

In 1963, tragedy struck. Myra's dear husband Moe suffered a ruptured aorta and died. Her sister, brother, and mother all died around the same time, also from heart disease. It was a terrible time, and Myra grieved deeply. But her work waited. As soon as she possibly could, she gathered herself together and carried on.

One of Myra's fiercest fights in the 1960s was with Detroit's Playboy Club, which had just opened. Waitresses there, or "bunnies," as they were called, would have no guaranteed salaries. To verify this, Myra sent her seventeen-year-old daughter in to ask for a job. Martha interviewed with the brother of Playboy founder Hugh Hefner. He offered Martha a waitress job, even though she was underage.

"You can make $250 a week," he told her—a fantastic wage for the time. "There is no need for a guaranteed salary."

Myra set up picket headquarters in a motel room near the Playboy Club. Two thousand picketers prepared for what would become the longest siege in Local 705's history. Through her network, Myra got church leaders to write letters to newspapers protesting the club. She kept the same newspapers informed about Playboy's archaic labor practices. "Playboy's no-wage policy makes the bunny beholden to the customer for her livelihood," she said, proclaiming that policy a "gross perpetuation of the idea that women should be obscene and not heard." Playboy offered a compromise: a guaranteed wage of ninety dollars a week if the waitress didn't collect that much in tips. Myra ignored the offer. How would such an arrangement be verified between management and the bunny who claimed not to have made that much?

In August 1964, television cameras captured the moment of victory when a sign that read UNION SHOP was placed in the front window of the only unionized Playboy Club in the nation. Myra and other picketers burned their signs in celebration.

Myra celebrated even more when Michigan's minimum wage law passed that same month. She stood in Governor George Romney's office in Lansing and watched him sign it. The hourly rate could be no less than a dollar an hour, and it would increase over the next two years.

Myra, later in life
—Michigan Women's
Historical Center and
Hall of Fame

After Moe's death, Myra found her way back to a vibrant life. She remained intensely involved with Local 705. She also worked with the Hotel Employees and Restaurant Employees International Alliance, for which she represented women members, and became one of ten union women to advise the U.S. Department of Labor. To her joy, her daughters lived not far away in Chicago, and she had a granddaughter. Myra had close, supportive friends—some of them male—and almost all of them from work. She also swam regularly at the YMCA for exercise and to ease her stress.

Still, Myra suffered problems with her legs and began to have headaches. On New Year's Eve 1975, she was walking a picket line at the Host International Hotel at Detroit's Metropolitan Airport. The other picketers noticed that she didn't seem her usual peppy self. She wouldn't admit to feeling ill, but the next morning, her secretary called Myra's doctor. Testing revealed a brain tumor, and Myra died within the month, only sixty-one years old.

At a memorial service at the Detroit Institute of Arts, union people and other Detroit leaders paid tribute to Myra's lifetime of service to working people. But Myra might have enjoyed even more the competition held in her honor a year later in California: the Myra K. Wolfgang Memorial International Waiters and Waitresses Race. In the race, contestants dashed a quarter of a mile carrying a tray with four full champagne glasses. The winner was the first to cross the line with sixteen ounces still in the glasses.

Waunetta Dominic —Michigan Women's
Historical Center and Hall of Fame

12
Waunetta Dominic

RIGHTS WARRIOR

"I'VE FOUND NOTHING'S EASY," Waunetta McClellan Dominic said once in an interview. Certainly that was true of her life's work, the struggle for tribal justice in Michigan. Her people were the Odawa, also called the Ottawa—the same tribe Magdelaine LaFramboise belonged to a century before (see page 13). Like Magdelaine, Waunetta (pronounced wah-NEED-a) devoted most of her adult life to improving the lives of her people.

Before European settlement, the Odawa lived a life of hunting, gathering, agriculture, and trading. In the summer they migrated into the northern part of Michigan. In the winter, they returned to the south of the state, a warmer, more protected place. The Odawa belonged to a federation of related Great Lakes tribes who called themselves the *Anishnabek* or *Anishnabe*—meaning the "Real People" or "Good People."

After more and more non-Indian people settled in southern Michigan, the Odawa stopped migrating south and stayed in the north. During the American Revolution, they sided with the British and lost. Afterwards, they signed a series of treaties that ceded much of their land and rights away.

Waunetta was born to Levi and Elizabeth McClellan in 1921 in Petoskey. Petoskey lies on northwestern Michigan's Little Traverse

Bay, not far from Mackinac Island. As a child, Waunetta attended schools in Petoskey. Then, when she was fourteen, her parents sent her to the Haskell Indian School in Lawrence, Kansas, where she boarded. Government boarding schools for Indian children had, in the previous century, cruelly attempted to root out students' home language and culture. Fortunately, times had changed, and Haskell was more progressive. Children from 120 different Indian nations gathered there, lived together in dormitories, and attended academically rigorous classes. They also worked in the school gardens and dairy, helping to raise their own food.

Waunetta returned to Michigan when she was eighteen and married handsome Robert Dominic in Lansing. Robert, several years older than Waunetta, was also an Odawa. Waunetta had met him at the pier in Petoskey, when both had gone to the lake to swim. After graduating from Central Michigan University in engineering, Robert found a job as a metallurgist with the Buick Motor Company in Flint, Michigan. The couple led a pleasant life. They started a family and looked forward to a vice presidency at the company for Robert in the near future.

In 1946, however, President Harry Truman signed a law that changed the young couple's lives forever. The Indian Claims Act gave Native Americans the right to sue the federal government for compensation for land taken from them in the past. Before 1924, Indian people had not had that right because they were not citizens of the United States. Then from 1924 to 1946, if they wanted to sue, they had to get permission from Congress. The new law would make the righting of past wrongs easier for everyone—the courts, Congress, and Indian people. An Indian Claims Commission in Washington, D.C., was formed to handle three levels of claims from Indian groups.

At the first level, a tribe or band (a band is a smaller branch of a tribe made up of interrelated families) would document their ownership of, or title to, specific lands. To do so, they used as many native experts, treaties, and facts as possible. The federal government would search for similar evidence, usually with the intent of proving a smaller area was involved. The claimants also had to prove that they were a legitimate, organized group. Once the commission agreed that the group was legitimate and had title to the land and once they had also settled on the land's boundaries, the value of the land had to be determined.

At this second level of claim, the group making the claim had to figure out the value of the land when the original transfer of ownership took place. They had to dig up old documents: land sale records, treaties, acts of Congress, and presidential orders. If the claimant was able to show that a tribe or band had been underpaid, they entered the third level of claim, in which they were compensated in cash for the difference.

In 1948, Waunetta and Robert piled their children in the car to visit her family in Petoskey. When they arrived, Waunetta's father met them with excitement. "We didn't know anything about [the Indian Claims Act]," Waunetta remembered. "He told us to take this stuff and read it. We did and we got interested." From then on, Robert and Waunetta gave the new law and its ramifications every minute they could spare from work and family. If they wanted to make an Odawa claim, they saw they would have to begin at level one. They also realized it would be better to live in Petoskey, so Robert resigned his Buick job and found work as a chemist at a Petoskey concrete plant. Suddenly, the five-year deadline they had to file the claim seemed like a very short time. But they were determined. Their ancestors had been cheated in treaties—paid pennies for land that should have cost dollars.

The Dominics pulled up stakes in Flint and moved to Petoskey. There, with Waunetta's father and other Odawa leaders, they organized the Northern Michigan Ottawa Association (NMOA), which held its first meeting in the Dominics' apartment above a grocery store. Twenty Indian people turned up. After listening to the young couple, some walked out. They didn't believe such a claim could succeed. Those who stayed offered ideas, which Waunetta wrote on the back of a roll of wallpaper. But even the ones who stayed were skeptical.

Unfortunately, the Odawa had heard talk about claims, compensation, and past wrongs before. Other people had come through before and talked about justice. They had collected money to go to Washington, kept the money, and never come back. They had been con men, not leaders; no wonder many tribal members had doubts. "They'd been fooled so much; had their hopes raised so many times," Waunetta recalled. In addition, many Indian people had an aversion to the idea of, in Waunetta's words, "the selling of mother earth. . . . What they didn't understand . . . is that it had already been sold. We were suing for additional compensation."

Another huge obstacle loomed: the burden of proving legitimate tribal membership. Federal agencies had been set up to supply services only to enrolled members of tribes or bands that lived on or

From left to right: *Waunetta Dominic; unknown woman; Robert Dominic*
—Courtesy Little Traverse Bay Band of Odawas

near a reservation. But that description fit only about 20 percent of Michigan's Native Americans. Eighty percent received few if any government services. Unless something changed, they might not be entitled to any money from a claim.

"We were convinced we were on the right track," Waunetta remembered. "The first thing we had to do was prove that there were Indians in Michigan and that they lived on the land they were claiming." The NMOA did this by dividing Michigan into eleven units, based on where the early Odawa bands lived. The unit where Waunetta's band had lived was Unit 1. Leaders elected from each unit represented the members who lived there and kept them informed. Now the hard work started. Waunetta and Robert wore out five cars crisscrossing the state to verify, one by one and family by family, that the Indians making the claim were indeed who they said they were and that they still lived on lands ceded to the United States. During this time, Waunetta and Robert had very little money, but they managed. People helped by buying them a tank of gas or feeding them.

Once they had traced and documented tribal members' bloodlines and property, the Dominics hurried into the next phase, which proved to be the most daunting. They had to check land records in every county seat of Michigan to find out the selling price of land ten years before and after two treaties, one in 1821 and the other in 1836. Waunetta discovered that, when they signed these treaties, her ancestors had received half a cent to seventeen cents per acre for land worth ninety-two to ninety-seven cents an acre.

The more the Dominics researched, the more impossible the project seemed. In addition, at some point the NMOA and its claim expanded to include not just the Odawa, but other Michigan tribes too. Fortunately, some Michigan lawyers took an interest and volunteered their help. There was also Dr. Omar Stewart, a white historical researcher who specialized in land valuation. He had spent three years tracing the whereabouts of thousands of Indian people in Michigan. His help would prove invaluable. For the monumental and tedious task of dredging through records across the state, the Dominics' righthand woman was fellow Odawa Marie Shenanaquet. Shananaquet took charge of the job in Michigan's northern half, including the Upper Peninsula.

In 1953, after years of frantic preparation, the hearing with the Indian Claims Commission was scheduled at last in Washington, D.C. Waunetta and the NMOA grew anxious and excited. At the last minute, Dr. Stewart asked Waunetta to type up some quick reference cards in case he needed them during the hearing. She typed nonstop for twelve hours until the cards were ready.

During the hearing, over the course of eight days, Dr. Stewart recounted Indian claimants' testimonials. The testimonials demonstrated the individuals' intimate knowledge of the land they had lived on for so long. They could say exactly how far you could throw a stone into the woods before it hit a tree, or how far you could see through the woods. They knew exactly how good a certain piece of land was for hunting or gardening, how many logs it had produced, how many deer lived there, and how the soil was. During his testimony about so many individual people and details, Dr. Stewart only needed Waunetta's reference cards twice to prompt his memory. "After all that time I spent on those cards!" she complained.

The results of the hearing were mixed. Of NMOA's eleven Michigan units, only one band of Ojibwa won a settlement—of $927,000—which they ended up waiting seventeen years to receive. It would be 1971 before the Indian Claims Commission finally awarded the NMOA just over $10 million. But problems with federal recognition of tribes and bands and what qualifies a person for tribal membership slowed the delivery of the money. Until the situation was sorted out, the government put the money in a trust for safekeeping. Finally, in 1998, some of it was released to various tribes and bands. By that time, the amount in the trust had grown to $70 million! As of this writing, problems with recognition have continued to keep some of the land claims money from being paid out, but all of it is supposed to be distributed by 2007.

Some government officials reportedly said that Indian people were badly organized. Waunetta took exception to this. "You can call us unrecognized, but don't call us unorganized. And furthermore, I don't care if you recognize *me* or not. Recognize my rights." The truth was, NMOA had a reputation as one of the best-organized American Indian groups in existence.

Waunetta was proud that NMOA championed the rights of nonreservation Indian people. "It's a matter of principle," Waunetta said. "Nonreservation Indians see no reason why they should move to a reservation to have recognition and rights." For a time, non-reservation Indians didn't have the same access to free health care that reservation Indians did, even though their tribe and ancestors had won these rights. Waunetta gave attention to this problem, especially since she knew the money for the NMOA's claim might be delayed for years. Due in part to her efforts, a new ruling made medical care at Kinchloe Indian Clinic in the Upper Peninsula available to nonreservation Indians as well.

Waunetta's activism extended to other areas. In 1960, at a national gathering of Indians in Chicago, she was struck by the number of well-educated Indian people from other states. She wondered why Michigan had so few. She drew one of the conference leaders aside to ask him about this. He told her about federal money available for college scholarships and how to apply. Back home, she quickly began the paperwork and procedures for getting Indian kids to college. By 1978, 650 young Michigan Indians had qualified for college grants, thanks to Wau-netta's efforts and help. Speaking from experience, she reminded students, "You must live in two worlds . . . education and keeping up with the times can be combined with the study of Indian history, art, and language."

Waunetta's father-in-law, Robert Dominic, served as leader of the NMOA for more than twenty-seven years. In 1976, when he died, the group elected Waunetta to succeed him. Her children were grown by then, and she stepped up to the presidency.

Waunetta first turned her attention to the issue of Indian fishing in the Great Lakes, a controversy that stirred strong feelings on either side. Indian people claimed that the treaty their ancestors signed in 1836 gave them unrestricted fishing rights. Great Lakes Indians traditionally used gill nets to fish. Fish can get into these nets through openings, but when they try to get out, their gills snag on the net and they are trapped. Sportsmen and commercial fishermen complained that gill nets catch and kill fish of all species and sizes, and that was bad for fishing in general in the Great Lakes. Michigan banned gill nets in 1966, but some Indian fishermen still used them—resulting in angry and even violent confrontations with sportsmen and state enforcement officers.

Waunetta stepped in to negotiate for her people. She kept track of what was happening in the courts and served as a channel of communication with the various sides. Though a federal court ruled in 1979 that the tribes could continue gill net fishing, the controversy didn't really end until 1985. Tribes and the state agreed to give sports fishermen rights to a southern zone of Lake Michigan and Huron, and Indians and commercial fishermen received rights to the northern areas of these lakes and eastern Lake Superior. In the year 2000, further negotiations gave tribes $6.2 million to build fisheries.

Over the years, Waunetta made many trips to Washington, D.C., to testify before congressional committees on Indian affairs. Toward the end of her life, she received awards and recognition. In 1978, the *Detroit News* named her one of its "Michiganians of the Year" for her activism. Waunetta commented simply, "I believe I am a go-between between Indians and the 'white people.' I have been trying to get both sides together. The more you understand each other, the better you get along."

Obviously Robert and Waunetta's six children—Robert Jr., Christina, Dennis, David, Brian, and Michael—grew up in an activist household. In the 1950s and 1960s, several of the children took part in traditional native dance troupes that toured throughout the state. They learned about their Odawa heritage. As adults, several stepped into important political and cultural roles in Michigan. Professionally, some also followed in their father's footsteps by choosing work in scientific fields.

On September 21, 1981, at only sixty years of age, Waunetta died of respiratory failure in Petoskey and was buried in Greenwood Cemetery. Throughout her life, she had spoken for the rights of her people as well as members of other Michigan tribes and Native Americans in general. Her voice may have been quiet, but she spoke with persistence, passion, and determination, and she made a difference.

Delia Villegas Vorhauer —Michigan Women's
Historical Center and Hall of Fame

13 Delia Villegas Vorhauer

LATINA CRUSADER

AS A MEXICAN AMERICAN growing up in the middle of the twentieth century, Delia Villegas Vorhauer knew the difficulties that minorities faced in America. But as a leader, she came to see how belonging to two worlds had actually enriched her. She recognized that the same rang true with other kinds of "difference"—for example, being a woman in a man's world and, later in her life, being a disabled person in an able-bodied world. Difference brought rewards along with challenges.

Delia was born in 1940 in the border town of El Paso, Texas. Half that city's citizens were of Mexican origin, yet segregation ruled, and Mexican Americans and Mexicans had few opportunities for education. Fate, however, had been kind to Delia. Her father, Bernardo, was a prosperous optometrist who fit people for glasses. Delia's grandfather had been an optometrist as well. A photograph of Delia at age nine or ten shows a slender girl in traditional Mexican dress—an embroidered blouse tucked into a long satin skirt—with a sweet, dimpled smile and waist-length pigtails.

Delia had two older brothers, Bernardo Jr. and Roberto, and an adopted sister, Rebecca. Delia was close to her father. "He took me for walks and talked to me about the sky and constellations, and about world events," she remembered. Delia's mother, Consuelo

Olivares Villegas, devoted herself to her family and her religion. But she also had passions outside the home. She worked with poor children and was a painter whose work was sometimes exhibited. One winter, *Life* magazine published photographs of a spectacular nativity scene she had created. Consuelo's gardens were delightful, especially the prize-winning roses.

Delia attended a Catholic school in the Mexican city of Juarez, just across the border from El Paso. When she was thirteen, she began to wonder if she might be sick. Her grandmother and some aunts had all suffered from diabetes, a disorder in which the body cannot make or properly use the hormone insulin, and Delia thought

Delia as a young girl
—Michigan Women's
Historical Center and
Hall of Fame

she recognized some symptoms. On her own, she pulled out some of her father's medical books and consulted them. Then she asked her parents for a doctor's appointment. The doctor confirmed Delia's diagnosis. She had diabetes.

Insulin is important for regulating blood sugar. The body turns food into glucose, or sugar, which it then uses for energy. Insulin is what breaks the glucose down, making it available to cells. If there isn't any insulin, or it's not functioning correctly, the glucose doesn't break down and high glucose levels in the blood can create havoc in the body. People with diabetes run the risk of heart or kidney disease, amputation of lower limbs, and blindness. Fortunately, diabetes can be controlled medically and through diet. Delia learned what kinds of foods were good for her and which ones she should avoid. Sugary or starchy dishes, for example, could put her into a coma and even threaten her life.

Delia got used to her serious health condition and caring for herself, and soon her life resembled those of most teenagers. It was a family tradition to attend El Paso High School—Bernardo Villegas had been the first Mexican American to graduate from there. Delia did well in school and became editor of the school's newspaper. Despite some advances Mexican American students had made, Delia recognized other ways in which they were still limited. "The Mexican girls could be elected as princesses but never queens," she remembered. "Many Mexican boys were good in sports, [but could not win scholarships] and could never dream of going to college, like now."

After Delia graduated from high school, her mother encouraged her to go away to Chicago to school. Her father wanted Delia to be a teacher, but her mother thought she should have the opportunity to make up her own mind. The Villegases had relatives in Chicago, so it wasn't a totally foreign place. Delia attended Rosary College in River Forest, Illinois. During college, her diabetes got worse, and she had to start taking insulin. The illness would be a major concern in her life, and she faced it squarely.

Delia chose sociology, the study of human social interaction and organization, as her major. When she graduated four years later, in 1962, she knew she wanted a job in the field of social work. It was a sizable field; individual social workers did all kinds of work. Generally, though, they all offered some sort of support to people in the struggle to improve their lives. Often, social work clients belonged to groups with particular needs—children, for example, or immigrants, students, or the elderly. Some social workers worked with individuals, others with groups or even whole communities.

Delia entered social work at the perfect time. American culture of the 1960s and 1970s was recognizing the need to reach out to special, often underserved segments of society. It had begun to pay attention to other groups as well, such as women and minorities. Customs were changing and being reevaluated. Social movements like women's liberation, black power, and feminism were on the rise.

Delia stayed in Chicago and accepted a job as a caseworker with the city's Social Services. The first two areas she worked in were adoption and child custody. In the first capacity, she helped match babies with couples that wished to adopt. In the area of child custody, Delia helped decide who would take care of children in cases of neglect, abuse, or abandonment. She investigated the situation and reported her findings to a judge. Home visits were part of the job. Delia felt comfortable traveling alone into poor, racially segregated neighborhoods. "I always felt a great sense of identity with other Mexicans and minorities," she said. The judge nearly always accepted her recommendations.

Delia also wrote a monthly column entitled "Servicio Social" for a Spanish-language paper. In the column, she answered letters from readers. In her next social work job, she would be able to focus her energy on helping Hispanic people in particular. In 1964, she was offered the job of director of the Federal Manpower Development Training Program for Spanish-speaking people in Chicago. Delia recognized a magnificent chance to make a difference for people she cared about deeply. She threw herself into finding jobs for Hispanics and teaching them how to keep those jobs. To her delight, most of the agency's clients were well prepared for work and learned quickly. Soon Delia's program was graduating 97 percent of its students and finding them skilled work (which usually pays better): business and clerical positions, mechanical jobs, welding, and more. For this, in 1967, Delia was thrilled to receive a presidential award from President Lyndon B. Johnson.

What accounted for Delia's success? It was as if she had a magic key with which she opened doors to America's working class for Hispanics. She happily disclosed her "secret": she insisted that people in her program learn to read and write in English. But Delia's warm personal attention and concern for each individual also played a part. She reached out, helping each person progress and develop in their own way.

In 1965, Delia met Bill Vorhauer in Chicago. Tall and attractive, with reddish hair and hazel eyes, Bill was the son of a German immigrant to Mexico and the United States and a Mexican mother, so, like Delia, he spoke Spanish. He was easy-going, smart, and funny. After dating for three years, Delia and Bill married in June 1968 in Chicago's Holy Name Cathedral.

Not long after their wedding, the Vorhauers moved to Boston, where Bill attended Harvard University's School of Education. Delia supported him with the salary she made directing a storefront school for three hundred inner-city children. As a volunteer, Delia helped organize the first citywide conference for Puerto Rican immigrants. Working with leaders from that community, she coached them in how to present their needs to Boston's government. One very concrete outcome of the conference was scholarships to Boston University for twenty young Puerto Ricans.

When Bill received his master's degree, he and Delia moved to Ohio. He found work in a school, while Delia directed a migrant resettlement program. The program helped migrant farm laborers from Texas and Mexico settle into the area and locate services they needed for their families. Delia drove workers and their families to the hospital, showed them how to manage their money, and helped in whatever ways they needed. She said the job "strengthened my resolve to fight for a more equitable and just arrangement for migrant women and men everywhere."

Always industrious despite her struggles with her health, Delia decided to go back to school for a master's degree in sociology. Daily she drove to class at Bowling Green University. To pay for her courses, she taught as an instructor. When she finished in 1974, Delia and Bill moved to Lansing, Michigan. It would be their home for the rest of her life. Here, at age thirty-seven, Delia founded a feminist Hispanic women's group, Mujeres Unidas de Michigan—United Women of Michigan. She got the idea for the group when she attended a statewide conference for Latin American women, or Latinas. At the conference, she took note of Latinas' huge desire and capacity to make their lives and those of their families and communities better. But in many Latin cultures, traditional roles for women did not include roles of leadership. Instead, women were supposed to defer to men and focus only on caring for their family.

But Hispanic communities needed their women's help now more than ever, Delia believed. Taking on leadership roles didn't have to mean abandoning one's family. If women played a more decisive part in their communities and society at large, their loved ones would benefit. In fact, Delia and others argued, the well-being of their families depended on women taking these new roles. Because white middle-class women had done much to shape the model of feminism that was spreading through America in the 1970s, it didn't always fit the lives of Latina women, but it still offered thought-provoking, valuable ideas. The founding members of Mujeres Unidas experimented with which parts of the model worked for Latinas and which did not.

It can be hard leaving traditional roles behind for new, uncharted territory. One of the main goals of Mujeres Unidas de Michigan was simply to offer mutual support for women who decided to make this journey. "We needed that support in personal growth and development," Delia said. "That isn't easy to do alone." Mujeres Unidas also strove to educate Hispanic women. The organization gave workshops about political organization, as a step toward getting more Hispanics elected. Women learned how to analyze prospective jobs, including nontraditional occupations and professions. They learned and thought about the changing roles of men and women in the household.

"If we can help our women manage a lifestyle better, that is our role. Whatever our members are, we support it," Delia said. Enthusiasm was high, but Delia and other founders of Mujeres Unidas recognized that the journey toward equality should be planned in easy stages. Hispanic women needed to feel they were maintaining their culture. "The overall theme is the role of women in the context of the family," Delia said. In an interview for a newspaper article, she added, "You don't have to negate your traditional role entirely in order to grow yourself."

The results of Delia and Mujeres Unidas's efforts became obvious in 1977. When forty-eight Michigan delegates traveled to the National Women's Conference in Houston, Texas, six were Hispanic women representing Mujeres Unidas de Michigan. It is possible or even probable that, just a few years before, there would have been no Michiganian Latinas at this conference.

Delia had had to do some changing herself. She had grown up in a household ruled by her kind yet dominant father. Like the women she counseled and supported, Delia got involved in the wider community. In the 1970s, she served on the Ingham County Women's Commission. In a 1978 issue of the national magazine *Redbook*, Delia was recognized as one of ten outstanding Michigan women who were "making it happen."

At the same time she was involved with Mujeres Unidas de Michigan, Delia worked with the State of Michigan Department of Education. In that capacity, she grasped the opportunity to write the state's first report on minorities in higher education. A survey and summary of the status of minority students in the state's colleges and universities, the report became a powerful model for keeping track of that status. The document became known as the Mason-Miller Report, named after the state education officials who presented it to Michigan school districts. It could more correctly have been called the Villegas Vorhauer Report, after its author.

Delia worked hard during the 1970s for Mujeres Unidas de Michigan and for the Department of Education. Meanwhile the state's Hispanic community increased by leaps and bounds, both in size and power. Because the state is agricultural, it drew migratory workers, and many Spanish-speaking migrants chose to stay.

By 1980, however, time and hard work had taken a toll on Delia's health. Because of cell damage from her diabetes, Delia's eyesight deteriorated to the point of legal blindness. She was only forty years old. For two years she endured a series of laser treatments, but they didn't help. Doctors offered her the option of a high-risk surgical procedure. It may or may not be successful, she was told. She chose to have the surgery.

For three weeks, she lay bandaged and healing. Certainly this time of waiting was a trial for her spirits. Would she be able to continue her work on behalf of women's and Hispanic equality? The bandages came off. The surgery had done nothing to help her vision. Vacillating between the desire to give up and never leave her home again and her usual inclination to conquer the world, Delia ended up rising from her bed. Her strong spirit won out.

Bill was a huge help. "I am very fortunate as I have my husband who has not just understood, but actually made the two of us a team. We face my blindness together." Slowly, Delia got over her fright at not being able to see. She learned how to "cane travel"—feel her way along with the help of a cane. She stumbled, and banged into furniture. Sometimes she fell. Cooking presented problems, but with special aids for measuring ingredients and markings in Braille on her kitchen appliances, she burned only a few meals.

A talking watch told her the time. Dressing wasn't difficult, but others noticed that once in a while her shoes didn't match.

Gradually, Delia realized that her life had acquired a certain unique richness.

> Being bilingual and bicultural is having access to two worlds. You can realize your full potential because you have two areas in which to develop yourself. You can draw on two cultures. Being handicapped is much the same.

Delia went back to work. She learned to use tape recorders to keep herself organized, recording reminders for herself of important chores, deadlines, and meetings. Soon, she was back up to speed—the same devoted reformer she had been before her blindness. "I don't feel defeated by my impairment," she said.

Delia accepted a new and challenging job as coordinator and program manager of an independent living program for Michigan Rehabilitation Services. Rehabilitation Services helps people with disabilities find jobs and live self-sufficiently, and centers for independent living were part of that effort. It was Delia's job to set these centers up throughout the state. They weren't residential, but instead were centers of information and support staffed by rehabilitation and counseling professionals. Among other duties, the staff evaluated clients' needs, helped place them in jobs, and stayed in touch with them. The centers Delia helped set up still exist. If clients can't pay, the services are free. The centers serve clients with a range of disabilities, from epilepsy and hearing loss to brain damage, back problems, and more. Delia worked in this position for seven years. Colleagues and clients alike found her presence both lovable and powerful.

What Delia had learned and accomplished in the area of rights for Hispanic women she now applied to working for disabled people's rights. Her new activism won her many awards. But by September 1988, a complication of her diabetes forced Delia to spend time on a kidney dialysis machine. When a person's kidneys fail, dialysis takes over the kidneys' job, filtering waste products out of the blood and returning "clean" blood to the body. Delia had to acknowledge the dismal fact: at only forty-eight years old, she needed to retire. More than a hundred of her friends and colleagues gathered at a retirement luncheon to wish her well.

Of course Delia didn't stop. Realizing the need, she started a support group for people with kidney disease in Lansing. By the following spring, when the director of the Michigan Commission for the Blind had to leave for medical reasons, Delia agreed to fill in. The new job put her in charge of 117 employees, 6 field offices, and a training center in Kalamazoo. It held a lot of responsibility. "She was frequently afraid," Bill remarked of this time, "but she said her prayers, dried her eyes, and pressed on." The commission was in good hands.

Finally, Delia could no longer work. In 1990, she and Bill moved to Las Cruces, New Mexico, to be close to her brother, Roberto, a Catholic priest. She died two years later at age fifty-two.

Destined to be brief, Delia's life nonetheless had profound impact. She recognized needs in her community and took action to meet them. She saw the potential in every human being and worked for fuller, richer lives for all. Time after time, she inspired those around her with her perseverance, dedication, and courage. But in her eyes, it was simple. "I've just had so many advantages all my life that I felt an obligation to give something back."

Bibliography

1. MARIE-THÉRÈSE CADILLAC

Bush, Karen Elizabeth. *First Lady of Detroit: The Story of Marie-Thérèse Guyon, Madame Cadillac.* Detroit: Wayne State University Press, 2001.

Dunnigan, Brian Leigh. *Frontier Metropolis: Picturing Early Detroit: 1701-1838.* Detroit: Wayne State University Press, 2001.

Galloway, Colin. "Abenaki." *Encyclopedia of American Indians.* Boston: Houghton Mifflin, 1996.

Harris, Fran. *Focus: Michigan Women 1701-1977.* Lansing, MI: Michigan Coordinating Commission of the National Commission on the Observance of Women's Year, 1977.

Hivert-Carthew, Annick. *Cadillac and the Dawn of Detroit.* Davisburg, MI: Wilderness Adventure Books, 1994.

———. Interview with author, January 10, 2005.

Landry, Peter. "Antoine De La Mothe Cadillac." Historical Biographies, Nova Scotia. http://www.blupete.com/Hist/BiosNs/1700-63/Cadillac.htm.

Middleton, Carol. "The French Colonials on the Gulf Coast." http://homepages.rootsweb.com/~cmddlton/colnls1.html.

Parkins, AE. *The Historical Geography of Detroit.* University Series III. Lansing, MI: Michigan Historical Commission, 1918. Reprint, Port Washington, NY: Kennikat Press, 1970.

Société du Musée Canadien des Civilisations, Virtual Museum of New France. "Lamothe Cadillac, 1694-1701." http://www.civilization.ca/vmnf/explor/cadie2.html.

Wallin, Helen. "Women of Michigan before 1840." *Michigan in Books 9,* no. 2 (Winter 1967): 43–53.

Woodford, Frank B. *All Our Yesterdays: A Brief History of Detroit.* Detroit: Wayne State University Press, 1969.

2. MAGDELAINE LaFRAMBOISE

Angel Fire. "Ottawa People/Anishnabe." The Pages of Shades—Native Americans. www.angelfire.com/realm/shades/nativeamericans/ottawa.htm.

Baldwin, James. *The Conquest of the Old Northwest and Its Settlement.* New York: American Book Company, 1901.

Cleland, Charles E. *Rites of Conquest: The History and Culture of Michigan's Native Americans.* Ann Arbor: University of Michigan Press, 1992.

Densmore, Frances. *Chippewa Customs.* Minneapolis: Ross & Haines, 1970.

De Tocqueville, Alexis. *Democracy in America.* London: Saunders and Otley, 1835.

Edwards, Elizabeth. "The Legend of LaFramboise." *Traverse Magazine,* June 1996.

Fuller, SM. *Summer on the Lakes in 1843.* Urbana, IL: University of Illinois Press, 1991.

Lueck, Jackie. "Heirloom Passed Down by Generations." *Redwood Gazette,* December 31, 2004. www.redwoodfallsgazette.com/articles/2004/12/31/news/news3.prt.

McClurken, James M. *Gah-Baeh-Jhagwah-Buk: A Visual Culture of the Little Traverse Bay Bands of Odawa.* East Lansing, MI: Michigan State University Museum, 1991.

———. *People of the Three Fires: The Ottawa, Potawatomi and Ojibway of Michigan.* Grand Rapids, MI: Grand Rapids Inter-Tribal Council, 1988.

Pierson, George Wilson. *Tocqueville and Beaumont in America.* New York: Oxford University Press, 1938.

Shellenbarger, Pat. "City Namesake Cast in Bronze." *Grand Rapids Press,* July 3, 2005.

Sleeper-Smith, Susan. *Indian Women and French Men.* Amherst: Massachusetts University Press, 2001.

"War in Michigan." *Insider's Guide to Michigan,* "Traverse Bay History." http://www.insiders.com/traverse/main-history2.htm.

Widder, Keith R. "Magdelaine LaFramboise: Fur Trader." In *Historic Women of Michigan,* edited by Rosalie Troester. Lansing, MI: Michigan Women's Studies Association, 1987.

3. ELIZABETH CHANDLER/LAURA HAVILAND

Dietrich, Emily. "Laura Smith Haviland, Emancipator." In *Historic Women of Michigan,* edited by Rosalie Troester. Lansing, MI: Michigan Women's Studies Association, 1987.

Edmund, Mary. "The G.R. Connection: Runaway Slaves Moved Through City." *Grand Rapids Press*, February 14, 1982.

Fields, Harriet. "Laura Haviland: Forceful, Fluent Humanitarian." *Daily Telegram,* June 26, 1975.

Filler, Louis. *The Crusade Against Slavery: 1830–1860.* New York: Harper & Row, 1960.

Harris, Fran, *Focus: Michigan Women, 1701-1977.* Lansing, MI: Michigan Coordinating Committee of the National Commission on the Observance of Women's Year, 1977.

Haviland, Laura Smith. *A Woman's Life Work.* Cincinnati, OH: Walden & Stowe, 1882.

Lindquist, Charles. Discussion and e-mail correspondence with author, June 1 and December 17–18, 2005.

Mason, Marcia Heringa. *Remember the Distance that Divides Us: The Family Letters of Philadelphia Quaker Abolitionist and Michigan Pioneer Elizabeth Margaret Chandler, 1830–1842.* East Lansing: Michigan State University Press, 2004.

Motz, Marilyn. *True Sisterhood: Michigan Women and Their Kin, 1820-1920.* Albany, NY: State University of New York Press, 1983.

Yates, Dorothy L. "Belles of Freedom: Three Women Antislavery Editors." Masters thesis, Michigan State University School of Journalism, 1969.

4. EMMA EDMONDS

Blanton, DeAnne. "Women Soldiers of the Civil War." *Prologue Magazine,* National Archives, Spring 1993. http://www.archives.gov/publications/prologue/1993/spring/women-in-the-civil-war.l.html.

Edmonds, Emma. Honorees file. Michigan Women's Hall of Fame, Lansing.

Edmonds, Sarah Emma. *Memoirs of a Soldier, Nurse and Spy: A Woman's Adventures in the Union Army.* DeKalb, IL: Northern Illinois University Press, 1999.

Harris, Fran. "What Was Her Reason?" *Focus: Michigan Women, 1701-1797,* Lansing, MI: Michigan Coordinating Committee of the National Commission on the Observance of Women's Year, 1977.

Jones, Thomas L. "The Women Who Fought in the Civil War." *Michigan Monthly Magazine,* January/February 1996.

Reit, Seymour. *Behind Rebel Lines.* San Diego: Harcourt, Brace, Jovanovich, 1988.

Smithsonian Associates. "Why Did Women Fight in the Civil War?" *Smithsonian Associates Civil War E-Mail Newsletter* 1, no. 8. civilwarstudies.org/articles/vol_1/woman.htm.

Stevens, Bryna. *Frank Thompson: Her Civil War Story.* New York: MacMillan, 1992.

5. LUCY THURMAN

Harley, Rachel, and Betty MacDowell. *Michigan Women: Firsts and Founders,* vol. 11. Lansing, MI: Michigan Women's Studies Association, 1992.

Hine, Darlene Clarke. *Hine Sight: Black Women and the Reconstruction of American History.* New York: Carlson Publishing, 1994.

Jones, Adrienne Lash, "Phyllis Wheatley Clubs and Homes." Reader's Companion to U.S. Women's History, Houghton Mifflin College Division. http://college.hmco.com/history/readerscomp/women/html/wh_028400_phylliswheat.htm.

McArthur, Judith N. "Woman's Christian Temperance Union." Handbook of Texas Online, Texas State Historical Association, 1997–2001. http://www.tsha.utexas.edu/handbook/online/articles/cite/handbook/online/WW/vawl.html.

Thurman, Lucy. Honorees file. Michigan Women's Hall of Fame, Lansing.

Winegarten, Ruthe. *Black Texas Women.* Austin: University of Texas Press, 1995.

Woman's Christian Temperance Union. "Crusades." http://www.wctu.org//crusades.html.

6. MARGUERITE deANGELI

Brunette, Joan. *Open Doors: A Biography of Marguerite deAngeli.* Lansing, MI: Michigan Women's Studies Association, 2003.

deAngeli, Marguerite. *Butter at the Old Price.* Garden City, NY: Doubleday, 1971.

Harrison, Larry. "Author Dead at 98." *The County Press* (Lapeer, MI), June 24, 1987.

Knight, K. Fawn. "Marguerite deAngeli: Writer and Illustrator for Children." In *Historic Women of Michigan,* edited by Rosalie Troester. Lansing, MI: Michigan Women's Studies Association, 1987.

Marguerite deAngeli Online Collection. Marguerite deAngeli Library, http://www.deangeli.lapeer.org/Books/.

7. PEARL KENDRICK/ GRACE ELDERING

Autumn, Stanley. *Mothers and Daughters of Invention: Notes for a Revised History of Technology.* New Brunswick, NJ: Rutgers University Press, 1995.

Draeger, Carey. "Pearl Luella Kendrick." *Michigan History Magazine,* May/June 1991.

Eldering, Grace. Honorees file. Michigan Women's Hall of Fame, Lansing, MI.

Greater Grand Rapids Women's History Council. "Dr. Pearl Kendrick and Dr. Grace Eldering." GGRWHC website, in "Projects: Seven Women Who Made a Difference" http://www.ggrwhc.org/proj-sevenwomen-kendeld.shtml.

Harms, Richard. "Grace Eldering Developed the Vaccine." *Grand Rapids Magazine*, March 1994.

Hopkins, Patrick D., ed. *Sex/Machine: Readings in Culture, Gender and Technology.* Bloomington, IN: Indiana University Press, 1999.

Hubred-Golden, Joni. "Researchers Linked to Whooping Cough Vaccine." Michigan Women's Forum website, vol. 3, no. 12. http://forum-online.info/HSArchive/HSElderingKendrick.html (June 15, 2006).

Kendrick, Pearl. Honorees file. Michigan Women's Hall of Fame, Lansing, MI.

8. GENEVIEVE GILLETTE

Dempsey, Dave. "The Lady of the Parks." *Michigan History Magazine,* September/October 2001, 13-26.

———. Transcriptions of interviews with Genevieve Gillette, 1975. Bentley Historical Library, Ann Arbor, MI.

Graham, Christopher. Telephone interview with author, February 18, 2003.

Jens Jensen Legacy Project, http://www.jensjensen.org/.

Johnson, Charles E. "Visit a Natural Area and Thank Genevieve Gillette." *Grand Rapids Press.* February 8, 1979.

Korn, Claire V. Phone interview with author, March 11, 2005.

Rutz, Miriam Easton. "Genevieve Gillette, Landscape Architect." In *Historic Women of Michigan,* edited by Rosalie Troester.

Lansing, MI: Michigan Women's Studies Association, 1987.

West Bloomfield Township Public Library. "Westacres Branch History." http://www.metronet.lib.mi.us/WEST/aboutus/westacres.html.

9. SIPPIE WALLACE

Alexander, Scott. "Sippie Wallace." www.redhotjazz.com/wallace.html.

George, Maryanne. "Detroit Has a National Treasure: Her Name is Sippie Wallace." *Detroit Free Press,* September 16, 1979.

Harrison, Daphne Duval. *Black Pearls: Blues Queens of the 1920s.* New Brunswick, NJ: Rutgers University Press, 1988.

MP3.com. "Victoria Spivey." http://www.mp3.com/victoria-spivey/artists/421/biography.html.

Peneny, Doug. "A Short History of the Blues." History of Rock and Roll website. http://www.history-of-rock.com/blues.htm.

Wallace, Sippie. Honorees file. Michigan Women's Hall of Fame, Lansing, MI.

10. CORA BROWN

Brown, Cora. Honorees file. Michigan Women's Hall of Fame, Lansing, MI.

Mayer, Michael S. "Ike in Office: The Tide Turns: African Americans Enter the Executive Ranks." *American Visions,* Feb-March, 1995. http://www.looksmartusa.com/p/articles/mim1546/isnlv10/ai16769674.

Swickard, Joe. "Black History Month: Detroit's Elite Are Buried at Elmwood." *Detroit Free Press,* February 14, 2005.

"Twenty-five African Americans You Need to Know." *Michigan History Magazine* January/February 2001.

Weeks. George. "Odd Bedfellows? Try Millikin-Jaye." *Detroit News,* May 17, 2001. politic/graveyard.comgeo/MI/ofc/stsen1950s.html.

11. MYRA WOLFGANG

Cobble, Dorothy Sue. "Lost Visions of Equality: The Labor Origins of the Next Woman's Movement." *Labor's Heritage* 12, no. 1 (Winter/Spring 2003). http://www.georgemeany.org/archives/featured11.html.

Cobble, Dorothy Sue. "The Prospects for Unionism in a Service Society." In *Working in the Service Society,* edited by Cameron Macdonald and Carmen Sirrianni. Philadelphia: Temple University Press, 1996. http://cpn.org/topics/work/prospects.html#6.

Davenport, Tim. "The Proletarian Party of America: 1920–30." Early American Marxism website. http://www.marxisthistory.org/subject/usa/eam/protelarianparty.html.

Fix, Janet L. "New Face of Labor." *Detroit Free Press,* March 24, 2001. http://archives.econ.utah.edu/mfem/2001m03msg00030.htm.

Harris, Fran. *Focus: Michigan Women 1701-1977.* Lansing, MI: Michigan Coordinating Commission of the National Commission on the Observance of Women's Year, 1977.

Pitrone, Jean M. *Myra: The Life and Times of Myra Wolfgang, Trade Union Leader.* Wyandotte, MI: Calibre Books, 1980.

Walter Reuther Library of Labor and Urban Affairs. "Myra Wolfgang Collection, Scope and Content." http://www.reuther.wayne.edu/collections/hefa1183.htm.

12. WAUNETTA DOMINIC

Cleland, Charles E. *Rites of Conquest: The History and Culture of Michigan's Native Americans.* Ann Arbor: University of Michigan Press, 1992.

Densmore, Frances. *Chippewa Customs.* Minneapolis: Ross & Haines, 1970.

Detroit Free Press, "Death Takes President of Indian Association." December 23, 1981.

Dominic, Waunetta. Honorees file. Michigan Women's Hall of Fame, Lansing, MI.

"Honoring Nations: 1999 Honoree." Harvard Project on American Indian Economic Development website. http://www.ksg.harvard.edu/hpaied/hn/hn_1999_land.htm.

Little Traverse Bay Bands of Odawa Indians website. http://www.victories-casino.com/tribal_history.html.

McClurken, James. *The Way It Happened: A Visual Culture History of the Little Traverse Bay Bands of Odawa.* East Lansing, MI: Michigan State University Museum, 1991.

U.S. Congress. House. *Michigan Indian Land Claims Settlement Act.* HR 1604 (Public Law 105–143). 105th Congress, 1st sess. (December 15, 1997)

U.S. Congress. House. *Michigan Indians Land Claims Settlement Act Amendments.* HR 4801. 109th Cong., 2nd sess. (February 16, 2006)

13. DELIA VORHAUER

Carter, Judy L., and Lenore Silvian. "Making It Happen in Michigan." *Redbook Magazine,* April 1978.

Vorhauer, Delia Villegas. Honorees file. Michigan Women's Hall of Fame, Lansing, MI.

Vorhauer, Delia Villegas. Primary Record Groups 01-1 and 01-2. Michigan Women's Hall of Fame, Lansing, MI.

Sites of Interest

GENERAL
**Michigan Women's Historical
  Center and Hall of Fame**
213 W. Main Street
Lansing, MI 48933
(517) 484-1880
http://www.michiganwomens
  halloffame.org

MICHIGAN HISTORICAL CENTER
Michigan State Archives
702 W. Kalamazoo Street
Lansing MI 48909
(517) 373-3559
http://www.michiganhistory.org

1. MARIE-THÉRÈSE CADILLAC
Detroit Historical Museum
5401 Woodward Avenue
Detroit, MI 48202
(313) 833-5342
http://www.detroithistorical.org

**Fort de Buade (Michilimackinac)
  Indian Museum**
334 N. State Street
Saint Ignace, MI 49781
(906) 643-6622

Madame Cadillac Dance Theater
(313) 881-8024
http://www.artservemichigan.org/
  members/mdecadillac

**Ursuline Monastery
  and Museum**
2 du Parloir Street
Quebec, Canada G1R 4M5
http://www.patrimoine-religieux.com/
  patrimoine_en.asp?no=22053

Statue of Marie-Thérèse Cadillac
Madame Cadillac Hall
Marygrove College
8425 W. McNichols
Detroit, MI 48221

**2. MAGDELAINE LaFRAMBOISE
Harbour View Inn**
P.O. Box 1207
Mackinac Island, MI 49757
(906) 847-0101
http://www.harbourviewinn.com

Averill Historical Museum of Ada
7144 Headley Street
Ada, MI 49301

St. Anne's Parish
P.O. Box 537
Mackinac Island, MI 49757
www.geocities.com/steanne2000/
  history.htm

**3. ELIZABETH CHANDLER and
  LAURA HAVILAND**
Catalog of Quaker Writings
http://www.qhpress.org/catalog/
  a-e.html

**Daughters of the American
  Revolution Museum**
1776 D Street NW
Washington, DC 20006
(202) 628-1776
http://www.dar.org/museum/
  exhibitions.cfm

**Lenawee County
  Historical Society**
110 E. Church
P.O. Box 511
Adrian, MI 49221
(517) 265-6071

Statue of Laura Haviland
Adrian City Hall
100 East Church Street
Adrian, MI 49221

4. EMMA EDMONDS
Historic marker
Genesee County Courthouse
900 S. Saginaw Street
Flint, MI 48502
(810) 257-3282

"A Nurse's View of Battle:
Bull Run, First Manassas"
Excerpt from *Nurse and Spy in the Union Army.* http://womenshistory.
about.com/library/etext/bl_
bullrun_001a.htm

"Women and the Civil War"
Dakota State University
http://www.homepages.dsu.edu/
jankej/civilwar/women.htm

5. LUCY THURMAN
Detroit Association
of Women's Clubs
5461 Brush Street
Detroit, MI 48202
(313) 873-1727
http://dawc.tripod.com

Historic pins made of stained glass
salvaged from the Lucy Thurman
YWCA are available for purchase at
the Detroit Institute of Arts (313-833-
7900) and at River's Edge Gallery in
Wyandotte, MI (734-246-9880).

6. MARGUERITE deANGELI
Marguerite deAngeli Branch,
Lapeer Library
921 Nepessing Street
Lapeer, MI 48446
(810) 664-6971
http://www.deangeli.lapeer.org

Marguerite deAngeli Online
Collection
http://www.deangeli.lapeer.org/Books/

7. PEARL KENDRICK and
GRACE ELDERING
Grace Eldering Collection
The Library of Michigan
702 W. Kalamazoo Street
Lansing, MI 517/373-1580
http://35.9.2.51/search~S34/X?
SEARCH=eldering&l=&m=&sear
chscope=34&SORT=D&Da=&Db

Medical Hall of Fame
Public Museum of Grand Rapids
272 Pearl NW
Grand Rapids, MI 49504
(616) 456-3977
http://www.grmuseum.org

Michigan Women and the
Whooping Cough
Vaccine Collection
Grand Rapids Public Library
111 Library St. NE
Grand Rapids, MI 49503
(616) 988-5400
http://www.grpl.org/collections/
grhsty_spcoll/finding_aids/328.
html

Pearl Kendrick Papers
Michigan Historical Collections
Bentley Historical Library
University of Michigan
1150 Beal Avenue
Ann Arbor, MI 48109
(734) 764-3482
http://www.hti.umich.
edu/cgi/f/findaid/findaid-
idx?c=bhlead&idno=umich-bhl-
85242

8. GENEVIEVE GILLETTE
Genevieve G. Gillette
Nature Center
P. J. Hoffmaster State Park
6585 Lake Harbor Road
Muskegon, MI 49441
(231) 798-3573
http://www.michigan.gov/
dnr/1,1607,7-153-10365_10887-
31270--,00.html

**Pictured Rocks
National Lakeshore**
N8391 Sand Point Road
P.O. Box 40
Munising, MI 49862
(906) 387-2607
http://www.nps.gov/piro

**9. SIPPIE WALLACE
Gravesite, Trinity Cemetery**
5210 Mount Elliott Street
Detroit, MI
(313) 921-0286
http://www.deadbluesguys.com/
dbgtour/wallace_beulah.htm

Online Discography
http://www.redhotjazz.com/wallace.
html

**10. CORA BROWN
Gravesite, Elmwood Cemetery**
1200 Elmwood Street
Detroit, MI 48207
(313) 567-3453

Michigan State Capitol
Capitol Square
P.O. Box 30014
Lansing, MI 48909-7514
(517) 373-2348

**11. MYRA WOLFGANG
George Meany Memorial Archives**
National Labor College
10000 New Hampshire Avenue
Silver Spring, MD
(301) 431-5451
http://www.georgemeany.org

**"Lost Visions of Equality: The
Labor Origins of the Next
Women's Movement"**
http://www.georgemeany.org/
archives/featured11.html

**12. WAUNETTA DOMINIC
Nokomis Learning Center**
5153 Marsh Road
Okemos, Michigan 48864
(517) 349-5777
http://www.nokomis.org

Haskell Indian Nations University
155 Indian Avenue
Lawrence, KS 66046
(785) 749-8404
http://www.haskell.edu/haskell/
about.asp

**13. DELIA VILLEGAS VORHAUER
El Paso Museum**
El Paso, TX
(915) 858-1928
http://elpasotexas.gov/history/

Paso al Norte Museum
www.pasoalnorte.utep.edu/overview.
html

**"Documents from the Women's
Liberation Movement: An
Online Archival Collection"**
Special Collections Library,
Duke University
http://scriptorium.lib.duke.edu/wlm/

Index